Interactive Notebook: Earth & Space Science

Authors: Schyrlet Cameron and Carolyn Craig
Editor: Mary Dieterich
Proofreaders: April Albert and Margaret Brown

COPYRIGHT © 2018 Mark Twain Media, Inc.

ISBN 978-1-62223-685-5

Printing No. CD-405008

Mark Twain Media, Inc., Publishers
Distributed by Carson-Dellosa Publishing LLC

The purchase of this book entitles the buyer to reproduce the student pages for classroom use only. Other permissions may be obtained by writing Mark Twain Media, Inc., Publishers.

All rights reserved. Printed in the United States of America.

Visit us at www.carsondellosa.com

Table of Contents

To the Teacher 1
Organizing an Interactive Science Notebook 2
Left-Hand and Right-Hand Notebook Pages... 3
Interactive Notebook Rubric.. 4

Interactive Units

Cover
What Is Earth and Space Science?... 5

Geology
Earth's Natural Resources 7
Earth Structure and Composition 9
Plate Tectonics 11
Types of Volcanoes 13
Earthquakes 15
Minerals.. 17
Types of Rocks... 19
Rock Cycle 21
Chemical and Mechanical Weathering 23
Soil, Erosion, and Deposition 25
Fossils 27

Oceanography
Ocean Water 29
Ocean Currents 31
Parts of the Ocean Floor 33

Meteorology
Earth's Atmosphere 35
The Water Cycle... 37
Factors Affecting Climate 39
Air Masses.. 41
Cold and Warm Fronts 43
Clouds and Precipitation 45
Air Pressure and Wind 47
Humidity and Dew Point 49

Astronomy
Our Solar System... 51
The Sun.. 53
Day and Night and the Seasons... 55
The Moon 57
Solar and Lunar Eclipses 59
Objects in Space 61

To the Teacher

The *Interactive Notebook* series consists of three books: *Physical Science, Life Science,* and *Earth and Space Science.* The series is designed to allow students to become active participants in their own learning by creating interactive science notebooks (ISN). Each book lays out an easy-to-follow plan for setting up, creating, and maintaining interactive notebooks for the science classroom.

An interactive science notebook is simply a spiral notebook that students use to store and organize important information. It is a culmination of student work throughout the unit of study. Once completed, the notebook becomes the student's own personalized science book and a great resource for reviewing and studying for tests.

The intent of the *Interactive Notebook* series is to help students make sense of new information. Textbooks often present more facts and data than students can process at one time. The books in this series introduce each science concept in an easy-to-read and easy-to-understand format that does not overwhelm the learner. The text presents only the most important information, making it easier for students to comprehend. Vocabulary words are printed in boldfaced type.

Interactive Notebook: Earth & Space Science contains 29 lessons that cover four units of study: geology, oceanography, meteorology, and astronomy. The units can be used in the order presented or in the order that best fits the science curriculum. Teachers can easily differentiate lessons to address the individual learning levels and needs of each student. The lessons are designed to support state and national standards. Each unit consists of two pages.

- **Input page:** essential information for a major science concept, instructions for a hands-on activity, and directions for extending learning
- **Output page:** hands-on activity such as a foldable or graphic organizer to help students process the unit

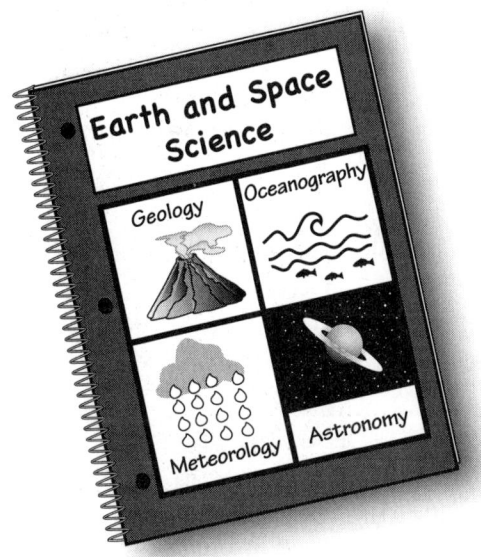
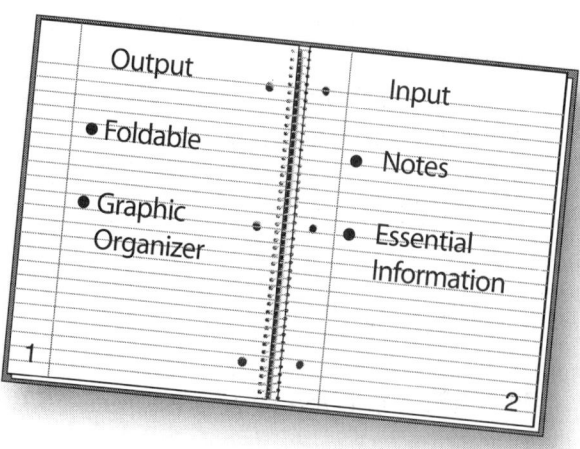

Organizing an Interactive Science Notebook (ISN)

What Is an Interactive Notebook?

Does this sound familiar? "I can't find my homework…class notes …study guide." If so, the interactive science notebook (ISN) is a tool students can use to help manage this problem. An ISN is simply a notebook that students use to record, store, and organize their work. The "interactive" aspect of the notebook comes from the fact that students are working with information in various ways as they fill in the notebook. Once completed, the notebook becomes the student's own personalized study guide and a great resource for reviewing information, reinforcing concepts, and studying for tests.

Materials Needed to Create an ISN

- Notebook (spiral, composition, or binder with loose-leaf paper)
- Glue stick
- Scissors
- Colored pencils (we do not recommend using markers)
- Tabs

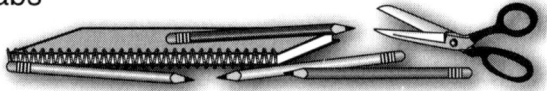

Creating an Interactive Science Notebook

A good time to introduce the interactive notebook is at the beginning of a new unit of study. Use the following steps to get started.

Step 1: *Notebook Cover*
Students design a cover to reflect the four units of study (see pages 5 and 6). They should add their names and other important information as directed by the teacher.

Step 2: *Grading Rubric*
Take time to discuss the grading rubric with the students. It is important for each student to understand the expectations for creating the interactive notebook.

Step 3: *Table of Contents*
Students label the first several pages of the notebook "Table of Contents." When completing a new page, they then add its title to the table of contents.

Step 4: *Creating Pages*
The notebook is developed using the dual-page format. The right-hand side is the input page where essential information and notes from readings, videos, or observations, etc., are placed. The left-hand side is the output page reserved for folding activities, diagrams, graphic organizers, etc. Students number the front and back of each page in the bottom outside corner (odd: LEFT-side; even: RIGHT-side).

Step 5: *Tab Units*
Add a tab to the edge of the first page of each unit to make it easy to flip to the unit.

Step 6: *Glossary*
Reserve several pages at the back of the notebook where students can create a glossary of science terms. Students can add an entry for vocabulary words introduced in each unit.

Step 7: *Pocket*
Attach a pocket to the inside of the back cover of the notebook for storage of returned quizzes, the class syllabus, and other items that don't seem to belong on pages of the notebook. This can be an envelope, resealable plastic bag, or students can design their own pocket.

Left-Hand and Right-Hand Notebook Pages

Interactive notebooks are usually viewed open like a textbook. This allows the student to view the left-hand page and right-hand page at the same time. You have several options for how to format the two pages. Traditionally, the right-hand page is used as the input or the content part of the lesson. The left-hand page is the student output part of the lesson. This is where the students have an opportunity to show what they have learned in a creative and colorful way. (Color helps the brain remember information better.) The lessons in this book use this format. However, you may prefer to switch the order so that the student output page is on the right and the input page is on the left.

The format of the interactive notebook involves both the right-brain and left-brain hemispheres to help students process information. When creating the pages, start with the left-hand page. First, have students date the page, then write the standards and learning objectives to be addressed in the lesson and the essential questions to be answered. Students then move to the right-hand page and the teacher-directed part of the lesson. Finally, students use the information they have learned to complete the left-hand page. The notebook below details different types of items and activities that could be included for each page.

Left-Hand Page Student Output (Odd-numbered pages)	Right-Hand Page Input: Teacher-Directed/Content (Even-numbered pages)
• State Standard • Learning Objectives • Essential Questions • Drawings • Diagrams • Illustrations • Graphic Organizers • Reflection Statements • Summaries • Conclusions • Practice Problems • Data from Experiments • Charts and Graphs	• Lecture Notes • Textbook Notes • Study Guides • Video Notes • Mini-Lessons • Handouts • Vocabulary • Lab Notes • Procedures for Experiments • Example Problems • Formulas • Equations

Interactive Notebook Rubric

Directions: Review the grading rubric below. It lists the criteria that will be used to score your completed notebook. Place this page in your notebook.

Earth & Space Science Interactive Notebook Grading Rubric

Category	Excellent (4)	Good Work (3)	Needs Improvement (2)	Incomplete (1)
Organization	Table of contents and glossary completed. All notebook pages numbered, dated, and titled correctly.	Table of contents and glossary mostly completed. Most pages numbered, dated, and titled correctly.	Table of contents and glossary incomplete. Several pages not numbered, dated, or titled correctly.	Table of contents and/or glossary missing or incomplete. Little or no attempt to number, date, or title pages correctly.
Content	All notebook pages completed. All information complete and accurate. All spelling correct.	Most notebook pages completed. One notebook page missing. Most information accurate. Most spelling correct.	Several missing or incomplete notebook pages. Most information inaccurate. Many spelling errors.	Many missing or incomplete notebook pages. Information inaccurate. Little or no attempt at correct spelling.
Appearance	Notebook pages very neat and organized. Writing and graphics clear and colorful.	Most notebook pages neat and organized. Most writing and graphics clear and colorful.	Notebook pages messy and somewhat disorganized. Writing and graphics messy. Limited use of color to personalize work.	Notebook pages very messy and lack organization. Writing and graphics illegible.

Student's Comments:

Teacher's Comments:

What Is Earth and Space Science?

Mini-Lesson

Read the following information. Then cut out and attach this box to the right-hand page of your science notebook.

Earth and space science is one of several branches of science. It is the study of the earth's physical structure, properties of the oceans, the atmosphere and weather forecasting, and objects outside the earth's atmosphere. Scientists investigate such topics as earthquakes, ocean currents, clouds, and asteroids.

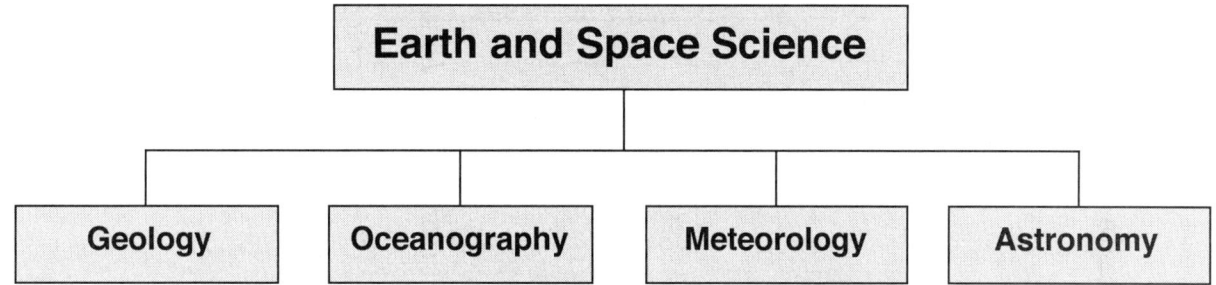

How to Create Your Earth and Space Science Notebook Cover

Create a cover that reflects the four units you will explore in your study of earth and space science.

Step 1: Cut out the title and glue it on the front of your science notebook.
Step 2: Flip through your science textbook to get an idea of the content you will cover as you complete your study of earth and space science.
Step 3: Fill in sections of the square with colorful drawings and diagrams that reflect the four units of study.
Step 4: Cut out the square. Apply glue to the back and attach it below the title.

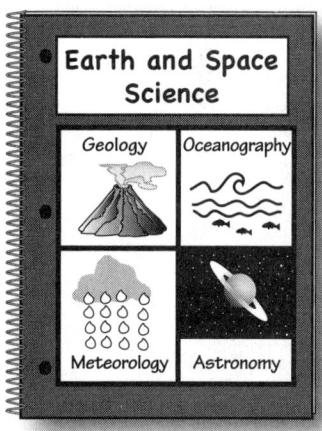

Reflect on What You Have Learned

Write a reflection statement on the left-hand page of your science notebook.

Question: What have you learned about earth and space science that you did not know before this lesson? Support your answer with examples and details.

Interactive Notebook: Earth & Space Science

Earth and Space Science Notebook Cover

Directions: Create a cover that will reflect your study of the four topics you will explore in your study of earth and space science. Fill in the sections of the template below with colorful drawings and diagrams. Cut out the title and template and glue to the front of your notebook.

Earth and Space Science

Geology	Oceanography

Meteorology	Astronomy

Earth's Natural Resources

Mini-Lesson

Read the following information. Then cut out and attach this box to the right-hand side of your science notebook. Use what you have learned to create the left-hand page.

Natural resources are materials found in the environment that are useful or necessary for people. Natural resources can be divided into two main groups: energy resources and material resources.

Energy resources are supplied by nature and provide people with energy. For example, sunlight provides heat and light; the sun along with wind and water can also be changed into electricity. Other energy resources include fuels such as coal, oil, wood, and gasoline. Energy resources can be classified as renewable or nonrenewable.

- **Renewable resources** are those that are replaced on a regular basis by nature. Animals, plants, water, and wind are renewable. For example, animals and plants can reproduce to make more of their own kind. Trees can be cut down and then new ones planted. Water and wind can be used to generate electricity.
- **Nonrenewable resources** can only be used once; they are not replaced quickly by nature. For example, coal, crude oil, and natural gas are considered nonrenewable because it takes millions of years for them to form.

Material resources are natural resources that include animals, soil, minerals, plants, and water. These resources can be used to make a variety of products. For example, wheat is ground into flour; sand is used to make glassware.

How to Create Your Left-Hand Notebook Page

Complete the following steps to create the left-hand page of your science notebook. Use lots of color.

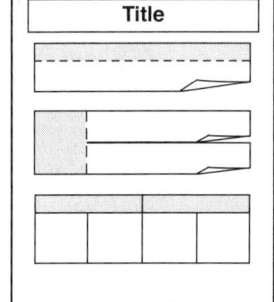

Step 1: Cut out the title and glue it to the top of the notebook page.
Step 2: Cut out the first flap chart. Apply glue to the back of the the gray tab and attach it below the title. Write the correct definition under the flap.
Step 3: Cut out the second flap chart. Cut on the solid line to create two vocabulary flaps. Apply glue to the back of the gray tab and attach it below the first chart. Write the correct definition under each flap.
Step 4: Cut out the third chart. Apply glue to the back and attach it at the bottom of the page.
Step 5: Cut apart the four picture cards and glue each card in the correct box on the chart.

Demonstrate What You Have Learned

Write a reflection statement on the left-hand page of your science notebook.

Question: Think about what you have learned and what you know. Would a rain forest be considered a renewable or nonrenewable resource? Explain your answer in your science notebook.

Earth's Natural Resources

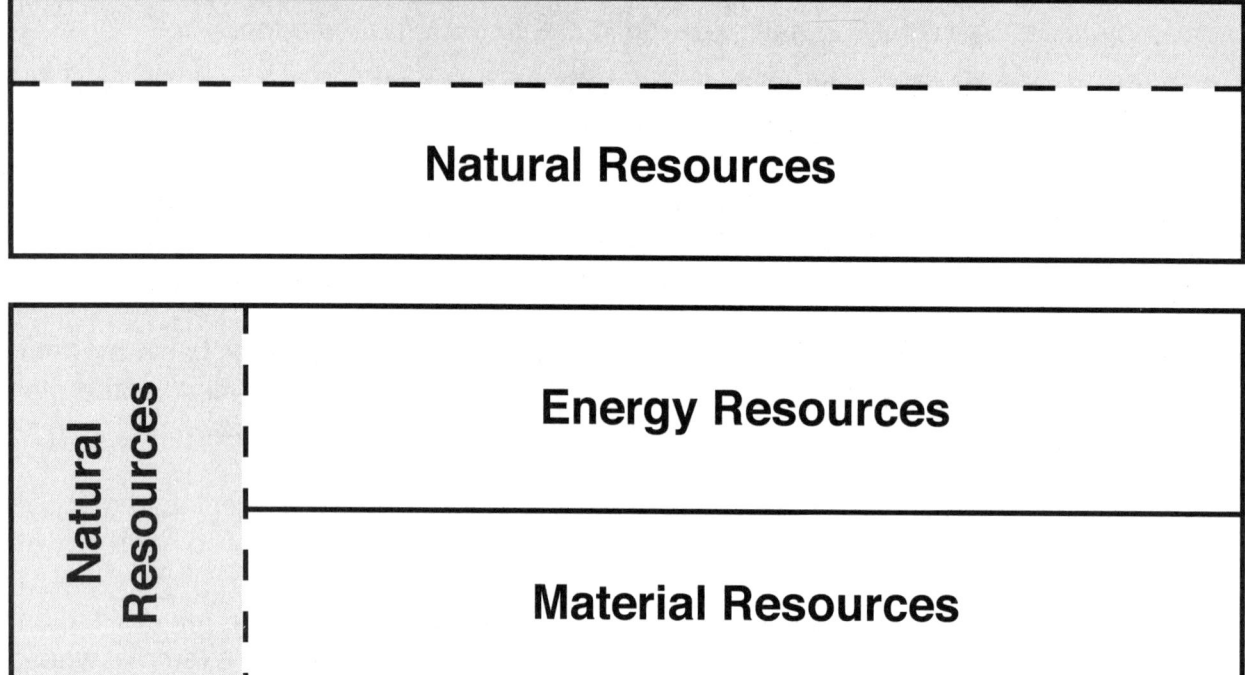

Renewable Resources		Nonrenewable Resources	

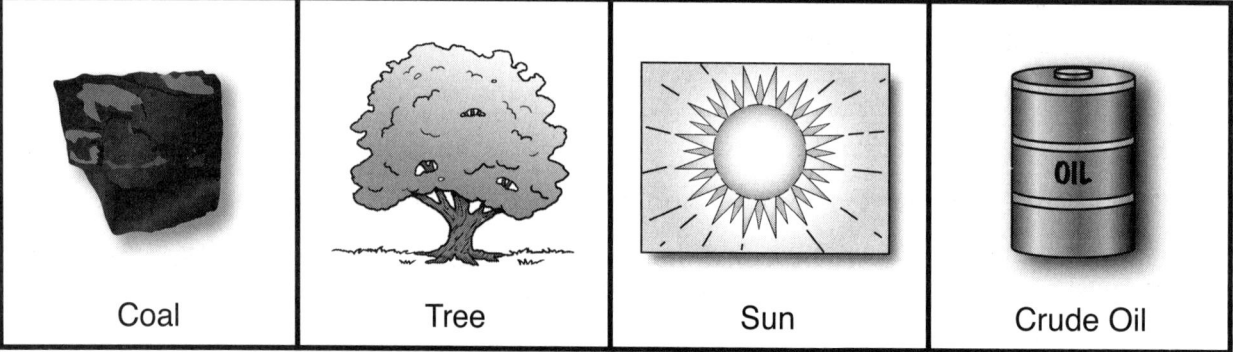

| Coal | Tree | Sun | Crude Oil |

Earth Structure and Composition

Mini-Lesson

Read the following information. Then cut out and attach this box to the right-hand page of your science notebook. Use what you have learned to create the left-hand page.

The earth is not a perfect sphere. It is a little flattened at the poles and bulges slightly at the equator. Earth has a rocky surface covered with a thin layer of soil, but beneath this solid surface, Earth is incredibly different. The earth consists of three basic layers: crust, mantle, and core.

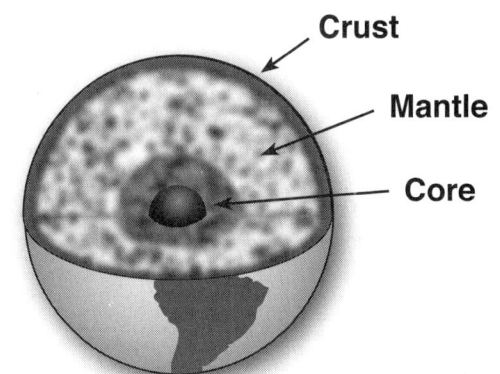

Compositional Layers of the Earth

- The **crust**, also called the lithosphere, is the outermost layer of the earth. The thickness of the crust ranges from 5 km (3 miles) to 100 km (62 miles). Some of Earth's crust is made of soil; beneath this soil is a thick layer of rock.
- The **mantle**, also called the asthenosphere, lies below the lithosphere. The mantle is the largest layer of the earth's interior, approximately 2,970 km (1,856 miles) thick. It is a hot plastic-like layer that surrounds the core. The upper part of the mantle melts rock, forming a substance called magma. According to the Theory of Plate Tectonics, the upper mantle provides the basis upon which Earth's plates slide.
- The **core** is the innermost part of the earth and consists of two distinct layers.
    1. The **outer core** is about 2,270 km (1,411 miles) thick. The outer core is composed of a liquid, mostly made up of iron and nickel.
    2. The **inner core** is solid, and is roughly 1,216 km (756 miles) thick. It is composed of solid iron and nickel.

How to Create Your Left-Hand Notebook Page

Complete the following steps to create the left-hand page of your science notebook. Use lots of color.

Step 1: Cut out the title and glue it to the top of the notebook page.
Step 2: Cut out the diagram chart. Apply glue to the back and attach it below the title. Correctly label the layers of the earth.
Step 3: Cut out the four word cards and glue each card in the correct box.

Demonstrate What You Have Learned

Create a three-dimensional model to show the structural and compositional layers of the earth.

Earth Structure and Composition

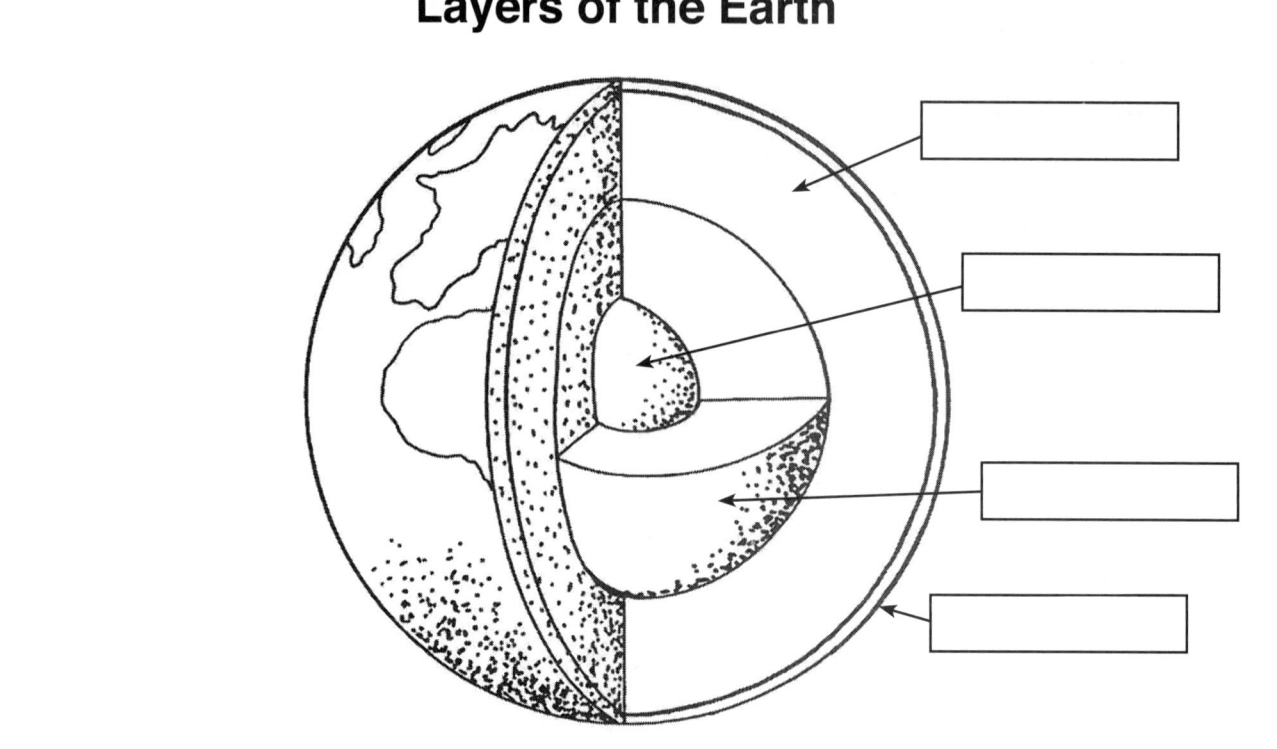

Layers of the Earth

Crust	Mantle	Outer Core	Inner Core

composed of solid iron and nickel	also called the asthenosphere, where magma flows	also called the lithosphere, composed of soil and a thick layer of rock	composed of a liquid, mostly made up of iron and nickel

Plate Tectonics

Mini-Lesson

Read the following information. Then cut out and attach this box to the right-hand page of your science notebook. Use what you have learned to create the left-hand page.

Plate tectonics and continental drift are both terms used to explain the present location of the continents. **Continental drift** is the theory proposed in the early 1900s that a supercontinent called Pangaea broke apart, forming the seven continents. The continents slowly drifted to their present positions. Today scientists use **plate tectonics** to explain how the continents were able to move to their present locations. Scientists believe the earth's outermost layer, the lithosphere, broke apart and formed seven large plates (pieces). The motion of magma in the mantle or asthenosphere, just under the crust, causes the movement of the plates.

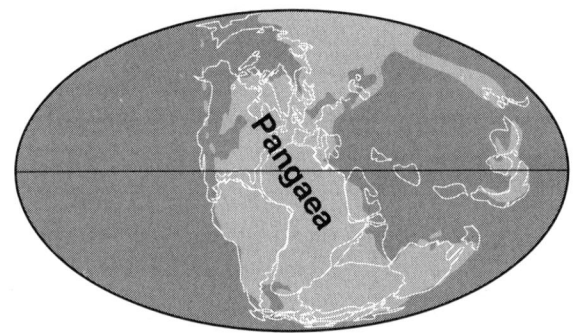

225 million years ago

The plates move between 5 and 10 cm a year. The plates sometimes collide and grind past each other at the plate boundaries. Earthquakes, volcanic activity, mountain-building, and oceanic trench formation occur along plate boundaries. Three types of plate boundaries are convergent boundaries, divergent boundaries, and transform boundaries. **Convergent plate boundaries** crash together, often forming mountains like the Himalayas and producing earthquake and volcanic activity. **Divergent plate boundaries** move apart. Most divergent boundaries are in the ocean. They build undersea mountain ranges called mid-ocean ridges. **Transform boundaries** form where two plates slide past each other, often causing earthquakes.

How to Create Your Left-Hand Notebook Page

Complete the following steps to create the left-hand page of your science notebook. Use lots of color.

Step 1: Cut out the title and glue it to the top of the notebook page.
Step 2: Cut out the flap chart. Cut on the solid line to create two vocabulary flaps. Apply glue to the back of the gray tab and attach the chart below the title. Write the correct explanation under each flap.
Step 3: Cut out the second chart. Apply glue to the back and attach it at the bottom of page.
Step 4: Cut apart the six picture and word cards and glue each card in the correct box on the chart.

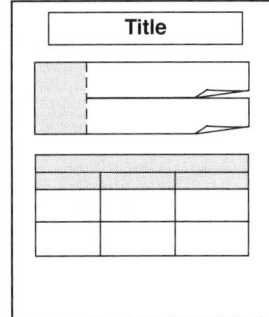

Demonstrate What You Have Learned

In your science notebook, give examples of where the three types of plate movement occur. Use your science textbook or online sources if you need help.

Plate Tectonics

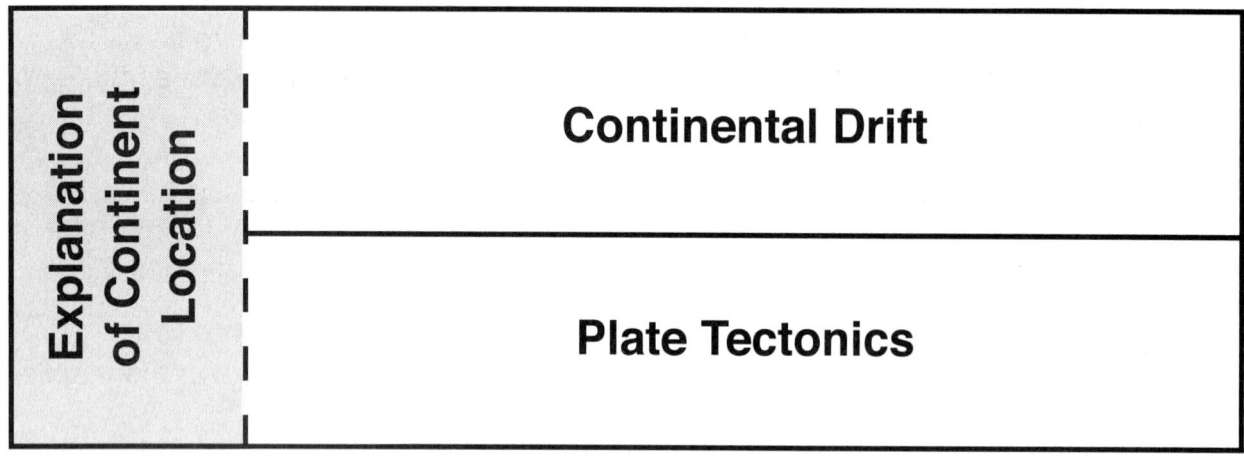

Plate Boundaries		
Convergent	Divergent	Transform

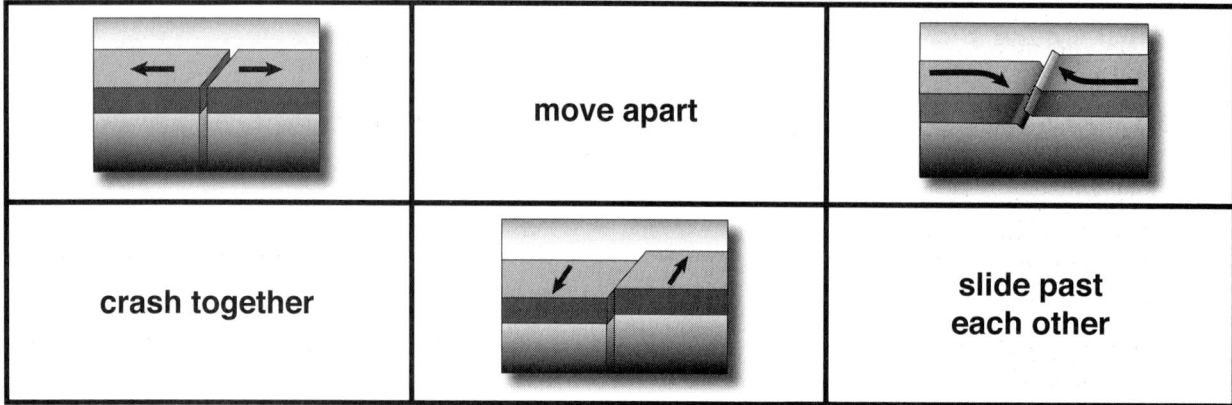

Interactive Notebook: Earth & Space Science Geology: Types of Volcanoes—Mini-Lesson

Types of Volcanoes

Mini-Lesson

Read the following information. Then cut out and attach this box to the right-hand page of your science notebook. Use what you have learned to create the left-hand page.

Volcanoes are vents (openings) at the earth's crust through which rock fragments, gas, and molten rock called **magma** erupts to the surface. The heat and pressure inside the earth becomes so great that rock melts. The magma is forced to the surface of the earth. Red-hot melted rock that comes out of the earth is called lava. The lava piles up, cools, and hardens, forming mountains.

A volcano can be extinct, dormant, or active. **Extinct volcanoes** show no activity and are often weathered down; scientists believe they will never erupt again. A **dormant volcano** is one that hasn't erupted for a long time, but it shows evidence of several past eruptions. It still has the potential to erupt. An **active volcano** is one that has erupted sometime during recorded history or is currently erupting.

Volcanoes can be classified into three groups based on shape and type of material they are built of: cinder cone volcanoes, shield volcanoes, and composite cone volcanoes.

- **Cinder cone volcanoes** have narrow bases and steep sides that built up when cinders (golf-ball sized blobs of lava) and ash are ejected from a single vent at the top of the volcano. Cinder volcanoes don't get very tall.
- **Shield volcanoes** form as layers of lava ooze out of the volcano and cool, forming wide thin layers that eventually shape like a shield.
- **Composite cone volcanoes** produce alternating layers of rock and lava. Shaped like a cone, composite volcanoes can grow into huge mountains.

How to Create Your Left-Hand Notebook Page

Complete the following steps to create the left-hand page of your science notebook. Use lots of color.

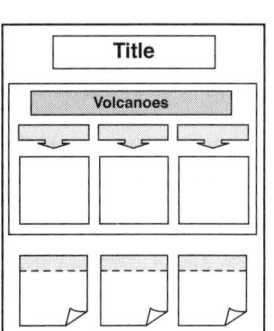

Step 1: Cut out the title and glue it to the top of the page.
Step 2: Cut out the graphic organizer chart. Apply glue to the back and attach the chart below the title.
Step 3: Cut out the three word cards and glue one in each arrow on the chart. Write the correct description in the box below each arrow.
Step 4: Cut out the three flap charts. Apply glue to the back of each gray tab and glue the charts at the bottom of the page. Write the correct definition under each flap.

Demonstrate What You Have Learned

Research the Hawaiian Islands. How were the islands formed and why are they unique? Write the answer in your science notebook.

Types of Volcanoes

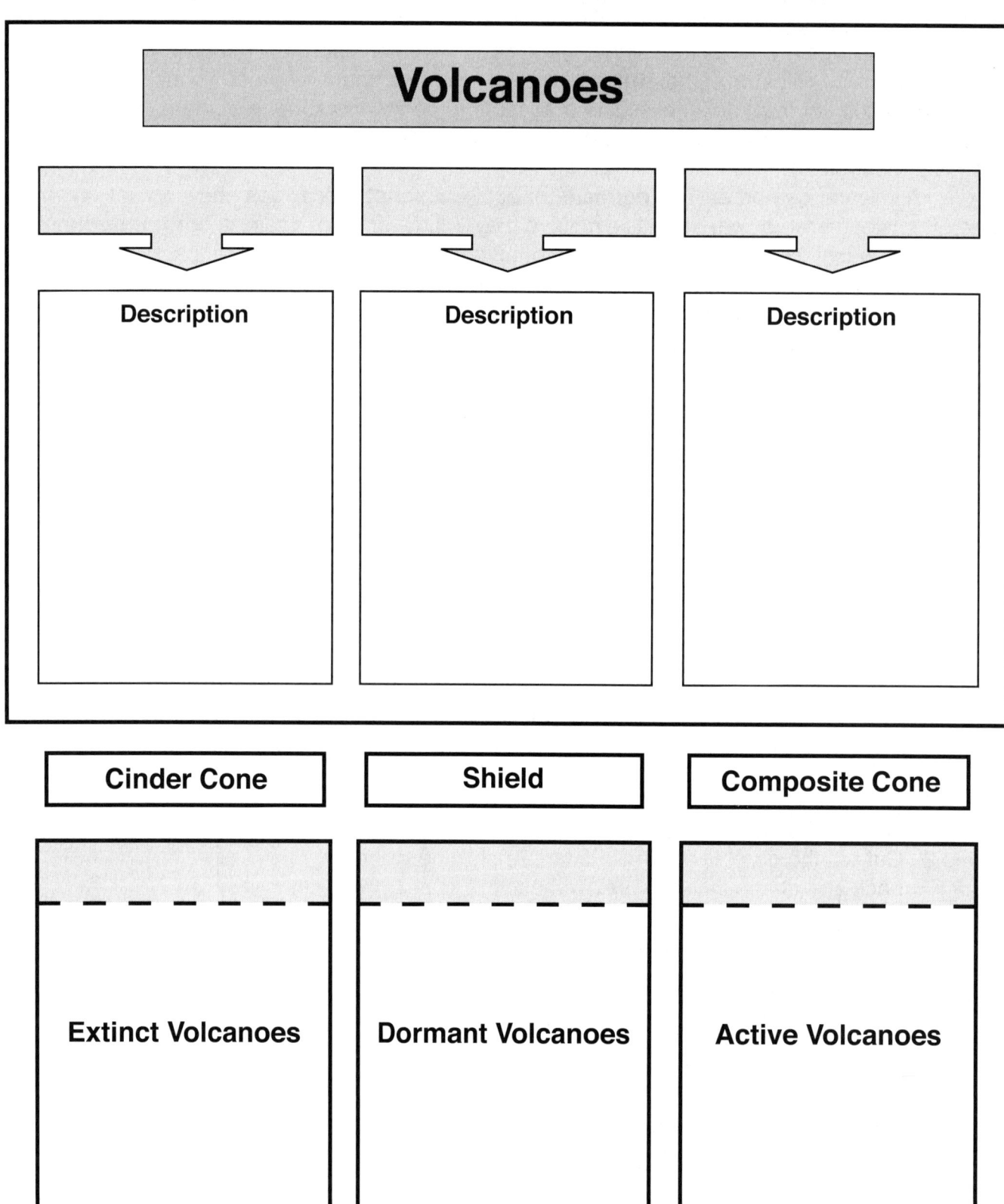

Earthquakes

Mini-Lesson

Read the following information. Then cut out and attach this box to the right-hand side of your science notebook. Use what you have learned to create the left-hand page.

The earth's crust is broken up into large sections that move. When two sections meet, pressure builds up. Where this happens is known as the **fault line**. When too much pressure builds up, the rocks suddenly slide past each other, and the pressure is released. The result is an **earthquake**. The place in the earth's crust where the pressure was released is called the **focus**. The focus can be many kilometers below the crust. Earthquake waves, or **seismic waves**, spread out in all directions from the focus. The earthquake's **epicenter** is the spot on the earth's surface directly above the focus.

The **magnitude**, or strength, of an earthquake can be measured with a **seismograph**. The **Richter scale** is used to gauge the magnitude of earthquake waves. The scale ranges from 1 through 9. Each number on the scale stands for a tenfold increase in the size of the wave. For example, a magnitude 6 earthquake has a wave that is ten times greater than a magnitude 5 earthquake.

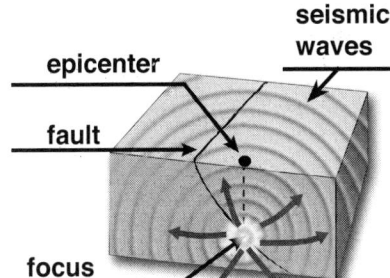

How to Create Your Left-Hand Notebook Page

Complete the following steps to create the left-hand page of your science notebook. Use lots of color.

Step 1: Cut out the title and glue it to the top of the notebook page.
Step 2: Cut out the diagram box. Apply glue to the back of the gray tab and attach it below the title. Write the correct definition for earthquake under the flap.
Step 3: Cut out and glue each box to the page. Draw a line from each box to the correct part of the diagram. Write the correct definition in each box.

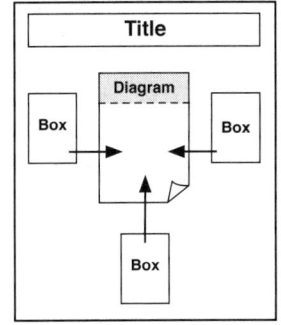

Demonstrate What You Have Learned

Research earthquakes and seismographs. Use the information to design a device that can be used to measure seismic waves generated by an earthquake.

Earthquakes

Parts of an Earthquake

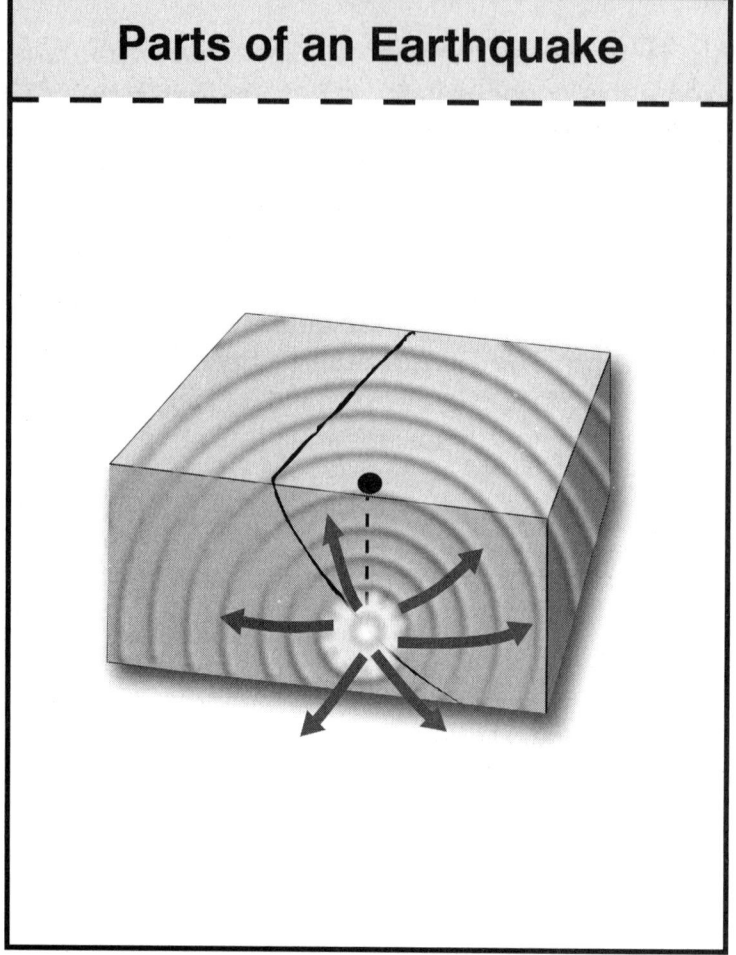

Focus	Epicenter	Fault Line

Minerals

Mini-Lesson

Read the following information. Then cut out and attach this box to the right-hand page of your science notebook. Use what you have learned to create the left-hand page.

A **mineral** is a naturally occurring, inorganic (non-living) solid with a crystalline structure. Crystals form in one of six distinct shapes. A mineral has a crystal structure even if it does not have a crystal shape that you can see.

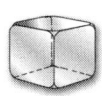  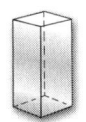   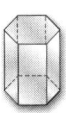

    Cubic   **Monoclinic**   **Tetragonal**   **Orthorhombic**   **Triclinic**   **Hexagonal**

Minerals can be identified by several physical properties. There are several tests that can be used for mineral identification.

- **Streak/color:** A test to identify the color a mineral leaves when dragged across a piece of white porcelain plate. The absence of streak should be noted as well.
- **Hardness:** A test to determine how hard a mineral is; the Mohs' scale consists of ten known minerals of varying hardness. The hardness of a mineral can be determined by rubbing an unknown mineral against the known minerals.
- **Luster:** A test to determine the way in which a mineral reflects light. Metals shine with a metallic luster. Nonmetals may appear silky, pearly, or dull, but never shiny.
- **Cleavage:** A test to determine how a mineral breaks; minerals that are considered to have good cleavage tend to split/break uniformly, along planes. Some minerals without cleavage break into jagged pieces.
- **Density:** This test refers to the weight of a mineral compared to an equal amount of water.
- **Magnetism:** A test to determine if a mineral contains magnetic properties; this is easily tested by placing the mineral near a magnet.

How to Create Your Left-Hand Notebook Page

Complete the following steps to create the left-hand page of your science notebook. Use lots of color.

Step 1: Cut out the title and glue it to the top of the page.
Step 2: Cut out the flap chart. Apply glue to the gray tab and attach it below the title. Write the name of the crystal structure below each picture. Write the definition for mineral under the flap.
Step 3: Cut out the second chart. Apply glue to the back and attach it at the bottom of the page. Complete the chart with the correct information.

Demonstrate What You Have Learned

Sprinkle salt on black paper. Examine the crystal shapes with a magnifying glass. What is the shape of the salt crystals? Write the answer in your science notebook.

Minerals

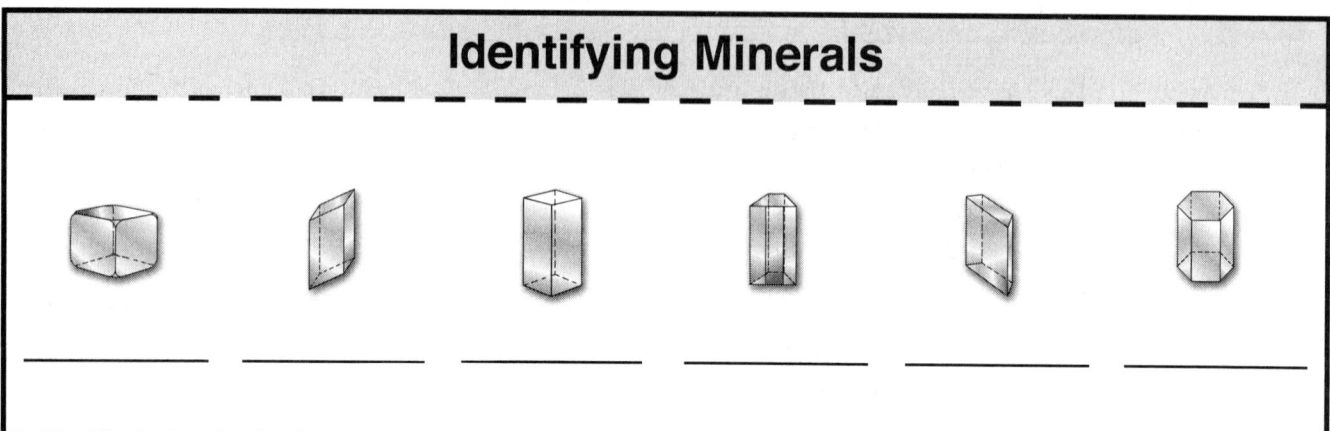

Identifying Minerals

Mineral Identification Tests	
Physical Property	**Definition**
color	
hardness	
luster	
cleavage	
density	
magnetism	

Interactive Notebook: Earth & Space Science   Geology: Types of Rocks—Mini-Lesson

Types of Rocks

Mini-Lesson

Read the following information. Then cut out and attach this box to the right-hand page of your science notebook. Use what you have learned to create the left-hand page.

The minerals formed deep within the earth combine in various ways to form the hard solids we call **rocks**. Geologists classify rocks into one of three groups based on how they form. These groups are igneous rocks, sedimentary rocks, and metamorphic rocks.

- **Igneous rocks** are also known as "fire rock." They are formed by the cooling of melted material such as magma inside the earth and lava above the ground. Rocks that form from quickly cooled lava are called **extrusive** igneous rocks. Obsidian is an example of an extrusive igneous rock. Obsidian forms when lava cools quickly above ground. Magma that cools inside the earth forms **intrusive** igneous rocks. Granite is an example of an intrusive igneous rock.

- **Sedimentary rocks** are formed when a layer of sediment (sand, clay, and other materials) becomes solid. Sandstone is a sedimentary rock.

- **Metamorphic rocks** are formed when sedimentary rock or igneous rock undergoes a change due to pressure or heat in the earth. Marble is an example of a metamorphic rock. Limestone changes under heat and pressure, transforming into a new kind of rock, marble.

How to Create Your Left-Hand Notebook Page

Complete the following steps to create the left-hand page of your science notebook. Use lots of color.

Step 1: Cut out the title and glue it to the top of the notebook page.
Step 2: Cut out the flap chart. Apply glue to the back of the gray tab and attach it below the title. Write the correct definition under the flap.
Step 3: Cut out the puzzle pieces. Match each vocabulary word with the correct description and example. Glue the matching pieces at the bottom of the page to create three complete arrows.

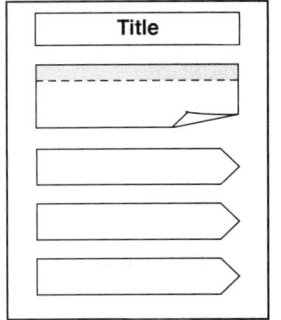

Demonstrate What You Have Learned

Create an edible model for each of the three types of rocks. Use online sources to help you find a creative idea.

CD-405008 © Mark Twain Media, Inc., Publishers

Types of Rocks

Rocks

Metamorphic > cooling of magma inside the earth and lava above the ground > 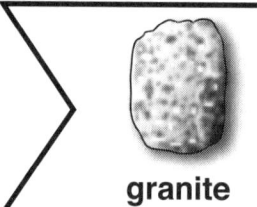 granite

Igneous > 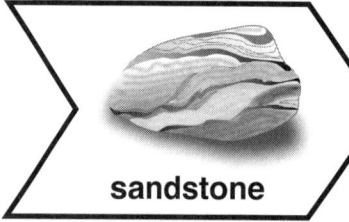 sandstone > a layer of sediment becomes solid

Sedimentary > sedimentary or igneous rock changes due to pressure or heat in the earth > 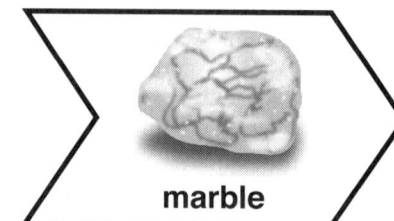 marble

Rock Cycle

Mini-Lesson

Read the following information. Then cut out and attach this box to the right-hand page of your science notebook. Use what you have learned to create the left-hand page.

Sedimentary, igneous, and metamorphic rock constantly and slowly change in form and structure over and over again as a result of natural forces. A diagram called the **rock cycle** is used to describe how different types of rocks are related to one another and how rocks change from one type to another through geological time. The rock cycle doesn't follow a particular order; it shows the changing and exchanging of matter through processes such as melting, weathering, erosion, and changing temperature and pressure. It is important to realize that rocks do not always go through all of the phases of the rock cycle. For example, igneous rocks may become metamorphosed beneath the surface of the earth without ever being broken down into sediment.

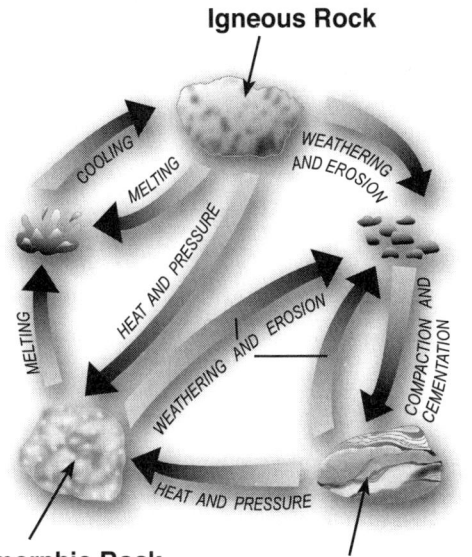

How to Create Your Left-Hand Notebook Page

Complete the following steps to create the left-hand page of your science notebook. Use lots of color.

Step 1: Cut out the title and glue it to the top of the science notebook page.

Step 2: Cut out the diagram box. Apply glue to the back and attach it below the title. Cut apart the three word cards and glue each card in the correct box.

Step 3: Cut out the flap chart. Apply glue to the back of the gray tab and attach the chart at the bottom of the page. Write the correct definition under the flap.

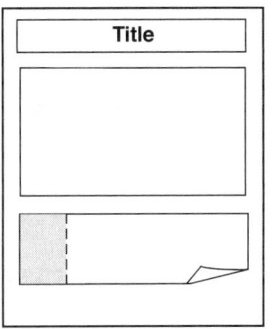

Demonstrate What You Have Learned

Research the rock cycle and use the information to create a poster that illustrates the cycle. Include the following information: 1) Describe the relationship between the three rock types: igneous, metamorphic, and sedimentary. 2) Explain how igneous, metamorphic, and sedimentary rocks are formed. 3) Explain how each type of rock is classified. Identify where igneous, metamorphic, and sedimentary are most likely to be found. 4) Provide a picture of each of the three types of rock.

Rock Cycle

Parts of the Rock Cycle

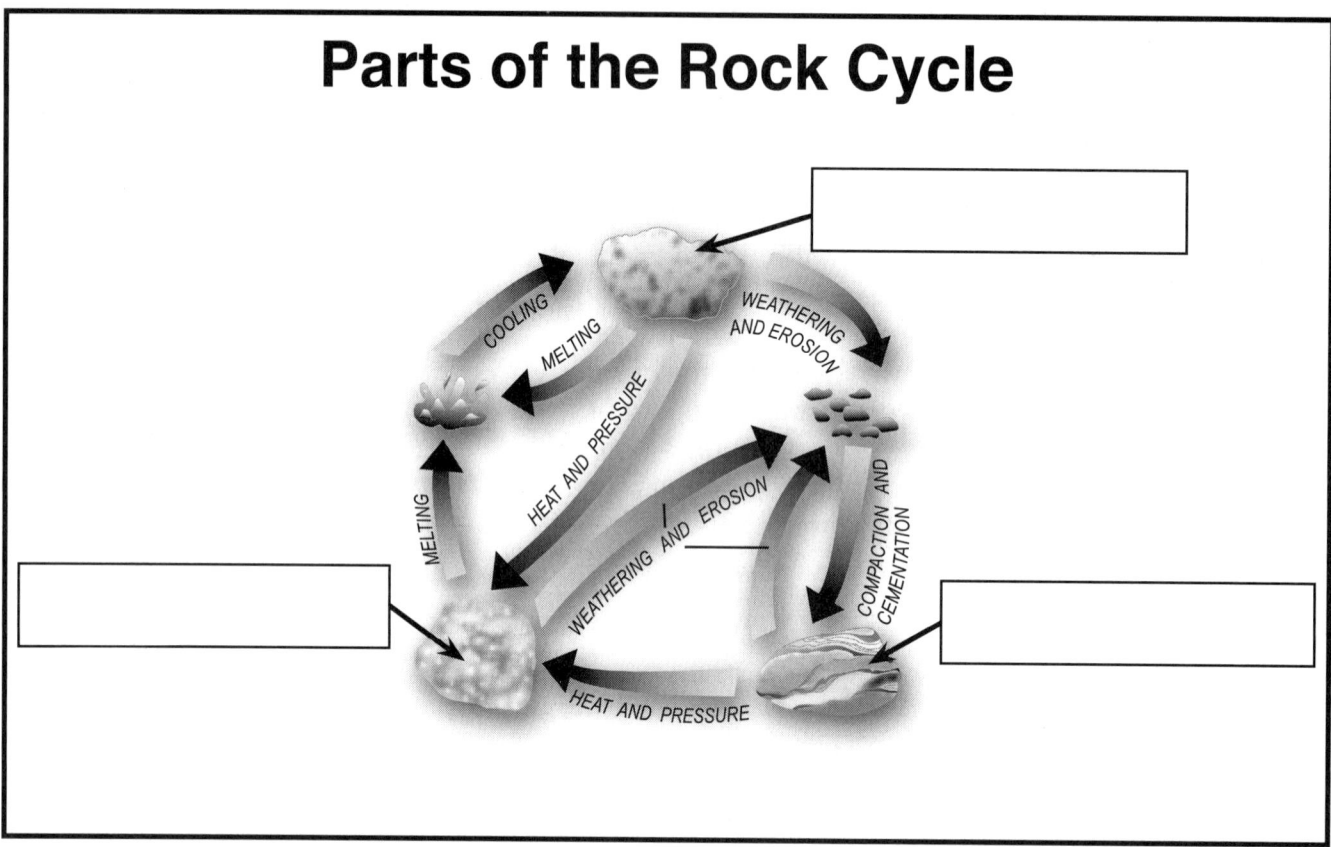

| Metamorphic Rock | Igneous Rock | Sedimentary Rock |

Rock Cycle

Chemical and Mechanical Weathering

Mini-Lesson

Read the following information. Then cut out and attach this box to the right-hand side of your science notebook. Use what you have learned to create the left-hand page.

Weathering changes the earth's surface over a period of time. It causes rocks to break into smaller pieces. There are two types of weathering: chemical weathering and mechanical weathering.

Chemical weathering causes changes in the chemical makeup of rocks and makes them crumble. Chemical weathering in caves causes stalactites and stalagmites. There are two main causes of chemical weathering.
- During oxidation, oxygen joins chemically with iron, forming red-brown rust; this is iron oxide. Oxidation weakens and crumbles rock as well as metal.
- Acid forms in rain, some plants and fungi make acids to carry out their life processes, or carbon dioxide mixes with water to form carbonic acid. Acid is responsible for the formation of stalactites and stalagmites found in caves.

Mechanical weathering is the breaking of rock into smaller pieces by physical forces. There are several causes of mechanical weathering.
- When water freezes in the cracks of rocks, it expands, forcing the cracks to open further and eventually breaking the rocks apart. Evidence of this process can be seen in the potholes formed in roadways.
- As the roots of plants grow in the cracks of rocks, the rocks break apart.
- Abrasion is weathering of rock through water and wind. Water carries sediment particles and wind carries sand that grinds against rock, chipping away the surfaces.
- Rain is another force that wears down rocks. The force of raindrops on some rocks makes them wear down and break apart over time.

How to Create Your Left-Hand Notebook Page

Complete the following steps to create the left-hand page of your science notebook. Use lots of color.

Step 1: Cut out the title and glue it to the top of the page.
Step 2: Cut out the two charts. Apply glue to the back and attach each chart below the title.
Step 3: Cut out the four picture and words cards and glue each card in the correct box on the charts.

Demonstrate What You Have Learned

Demonstrate weathering. Using two antacid tablets, break one up with your hands, and dissolve the other in a cup of water. How does this activity represent chemical and mechanical weathering? Write the answer in your science notebook.

Chemical and Mechanical Weathering

Chemical Weathering

Mechanical Weathering

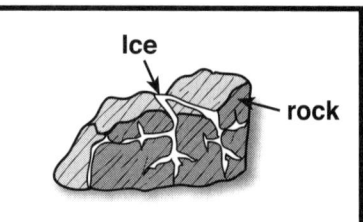

Changes in the chemical makeup of rocks cause them to break into smaller pieces.

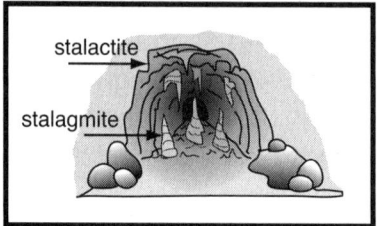

Physical forces cause rocks to break into smaller pieces

Soil, Erosion, and Deposition

Soil Horizons

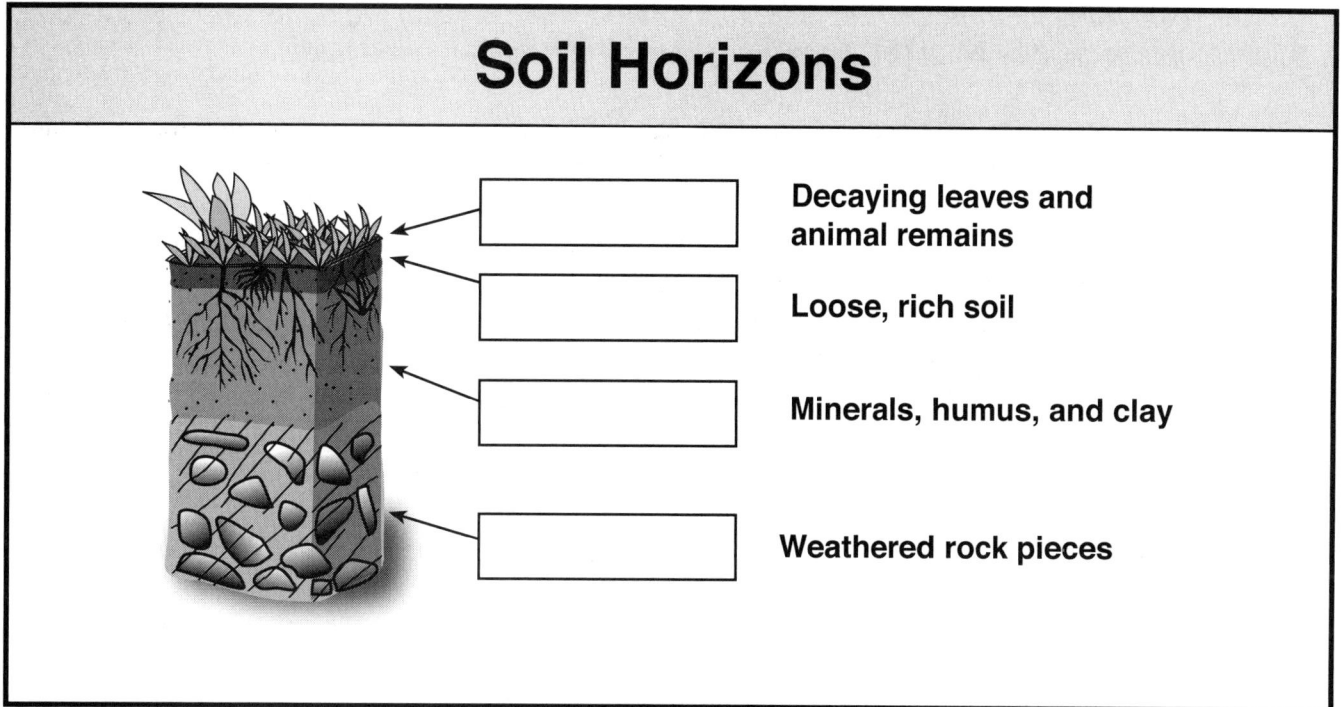

- Decaying leaves and animal remains
- Loose, rich soil
- Minerals, humus, and clay
- Weathered rock pieces

Weathering, Erosion, and Deposition

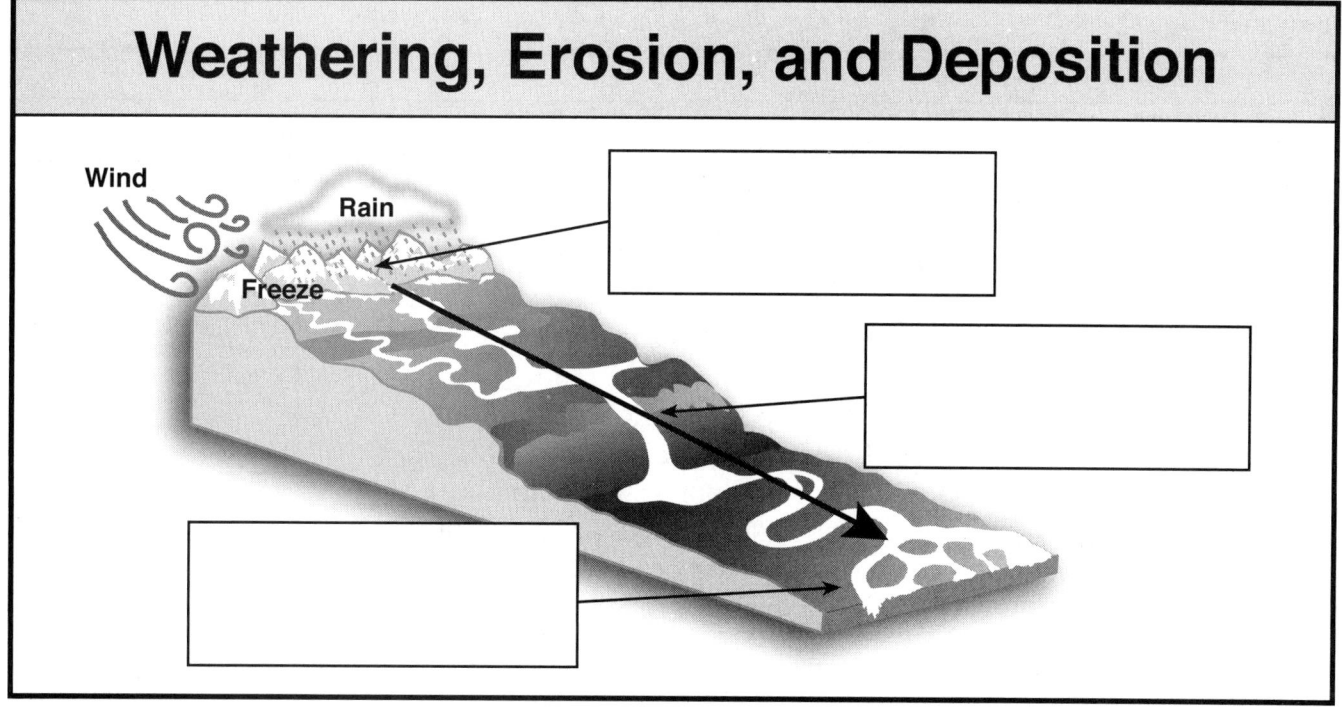

Deposition
material deposited in a new location

Weathering
wind, rain, and freezing break up rock

Erosion
rocks and sediments picked up and transported

Soil, Erosion, and Deposition

Mini-Lesson

Read the following information. Then cut out and attach this box to the right-hand side of your science notebook. Use what you have learned to create the left-hand page.

All life on earth depends on the soil. **Soil** is a mixture of nonliving things, such as sand grains, smaller rock particles, and minerals. It contains organic material that comes from decaying dead plants and animals. It also holds living things, both plants and animals. There are many different types of soil, and each one has unique characteristics. Soil forms distinct layers know as horizons.

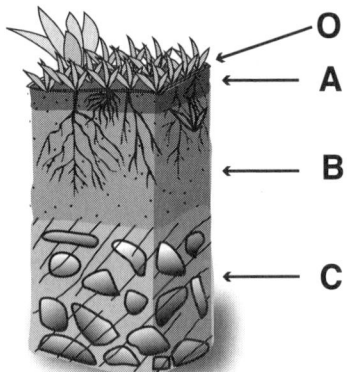

- **Horizon O:** layer of decaying plants, animals, and waste
- **Horizon A (topsoil):** layer of loose soil rich in materials plants need
- **Horizon B:** layer rich in minerals and also contains humus and clay
- **Horizon C:** pieces of weathered rock

Rock can be broken down to form soil by the process of **weathering**. **Erosion** happens when rocks and soil are picked up and transported to another place by ice, water, wind, or gravity. When these materials are deposited in a new location, it is called **deposition**.

How to Create Your Left-Hand Notebook Page

Complete the following steps to create the left-hand page of your science notebook. Use lots of color.

Step 1: Cut out the title and glue it to the top of the notebook page.
Step 2: Cut out the first diagram box. Apply glue to the back and attach it below the title. Correctly label each soil layer.
Step 3: Cut out the second diagram box. Apply glue to the back and attach it beneath the first diagram. Cut apart the three word cards and glue each card in the correct box on the diagram.

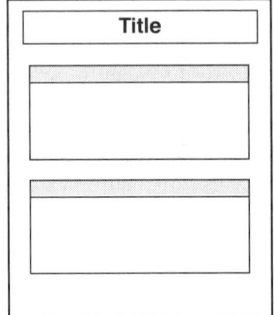

Demonstrate What You Have Learned

Design a working model of a stream system that demonstrates the process of erosion, transportation, and deposition.

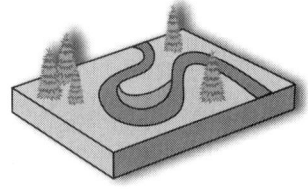

Interactive Notebook: Earth & Space Science   Geology: Fossils—Mini-Lesson

Fossils

Mini-Lesson

Read the following information. Then cut out and attach this box to the right-hand page of your science notebook. Use what you have learned to create the left-hand page.

Paleontologists study fossils to reconstruct Earth's living past. **Fossils** are the preserved remains, impressions, or traces of animals, plants, and other organisms. Fossils provide clues to 99% of Earth's organisms that have become extinct (no longer exist).

Fossils can be formed in several ways. Occasionally, entire organisms are preserved in some type of material. For example, insects encased in amber, resins from trees, become fossilized. Giant wooly mammoths have been discovered in the frozen tundra of the north. More typical are fossil remains of the hard parts of animals. Fossils form mainly in sedimentary rock. The skeletal remains (shells, bones, teeth) of living organisms are surrounded by sediment that settles on the bottom of a body of water, and the remains become trapped when the sediments harden into rock. There are six types of fossils.

- **Imprints** are impressions of parts of organisms left in sediment before the sediment hardens.
- **Petrified fossils** form when minerals replace the hard parts (teeth, bone, shell) of animals or plants, turning them into rock.
- **Mold fossils** are impressions left by plants and animals in a rock after the plants or animals have decayed.
- **Cast fossils** form when minerals collect in the mold of what was the plant or animal, forming a cast, or model of the original organism.
- **Coprolite** is animal dung that is petrified or turned into rock.
- **Trace fossils** consist of the footprints, tracks, trails, and burrows made by living things.

How to Create Your Left-Hand Notebook Page

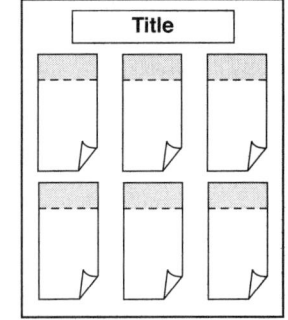

Complete the following steps to create the left-hand page of your science notebook. Use lots of color.

Step 1: Cut out the title and glue it to the top of the page.
Step 2: Cut out the six flap charts. Apply glue to the back of each gray tab and attach the charts below the title.
Step 3: Write the correct description under each flap.

Demonstrate What You Have Learned

Create a fossil imprint. In a large bowl, place 1,000 mL of flour and 250 mL of salt. Add 1.5 mL of warm water and mix, using your hands to form dough. Place dough on a hard surface and knead it until it is smooth and rubbery. Take a handful of dough and place it on a sheet of wax paper. Using a rolling pin, roll the dough to 1 cm thickness. Choose an item to be imprinted, such as a shell or leaf, and place it on the dough. Place a sheet of waxed paper over the objects and gently roll over the top of the objects with a rolling pin. Remove the waxed paper and item used for imprinting. Place the mold on a cookie sheet. Bake at 250°F in an oven until hard.

Fossils

Trace Fossils
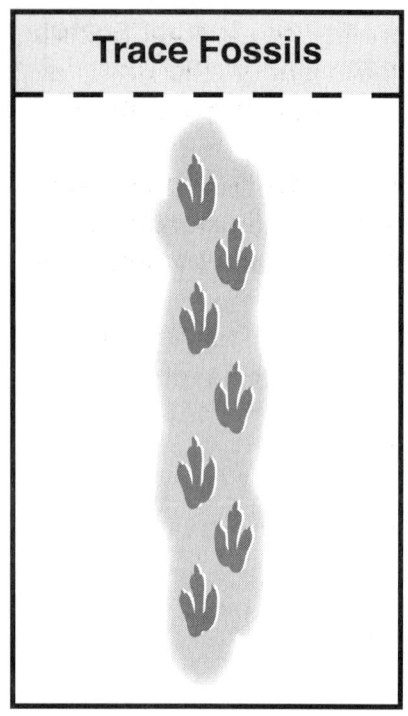

Mold Fossils

Cast Fossils
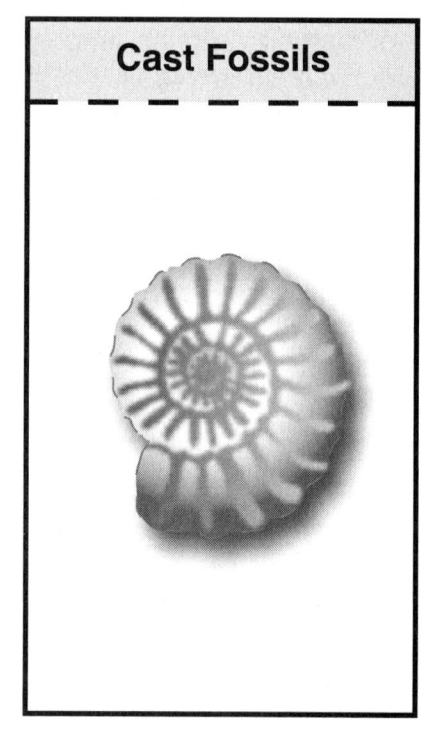

Petrified Fossils

Imprints

Coprolites
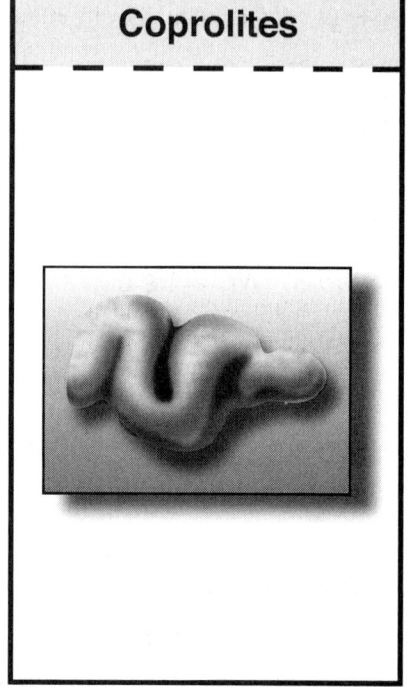

Ocean Water

Mini-Lesson

Read the following information. Then cut out and attach this box to the right-hand page of your science notebook. Use what you have learned to create the left-hand page.

Ocean water covers almost three-fourths of Earth's surface. The activity of the water cycle concentrates the ocean salts as the sun's heat evaporates water from the surface of the ocean, leaving the salts behind. The saltiness or **salinity** affects some of the physical properties of ocean water, especially density. Because ocean water holds dissolved salts, it is denser than fresh water.

The temperature of ocean water varies. The warmest water is at the ocean surface. Water temperature gets colder as the depth of the water increases. Generally, ocean water temperatures are warmer in summer than winter, near the equator, and in currents flowing from the equator than in currents flowing from the poles.

Oceanographers have divided the ocean into vertical and horizontal zones to make it easier to study individual areas. Major vertical zones of the ocean begin at sea level and end at the deepest points in the ocean. The small surface zone that has light is the **photic zone**. The entire rest of the ocean does not have light and is the **aphotic zone**. Most of the life forms in the oceans live in, or at least visit, the surface.

There are three main horizontal zones. The **intertidal zone** is part of the shore that is between the high and low tide lines. It is covered by water at high tide and open to the air at low tide. Organisms such as starfish, sea anemones, and crabs live in this zone. The **neritic zone** extends out from the intertidal zone across the continental shelf. The depth of the zone is up to 200 meters. It has stable temperature and salinity levels. Organisms such as plankton, lobsters, and fish live in this zone. The **open-ocean zone** is part of the ocean above the continental slope and the deep ocean floor. It has depths of up to 6,000 meters, temperatures in the deepest part are just above freezing, and water pressure increases greatly with depth. Large organisms such as whales, dolphins, seals, and tuna live in this zone.

How to Create Your Left-Hand Notebook Page

Complete the following steps to create the left-hand page of your science notebook. Use lots of color.

Step 1: Cut out the title and glue it to the top of the notebook page.
Step 2: Cut out the diagram box. Apply glue to the back of the box and attach below the title. Label each part of the diagram.
Step 3: Cut out the flap chart. Cut on the solid lines to create five vocabulary flaps. Apply glue to the back of the gray tab and attach it at the bottom of the page. Write the correct description under each flap.

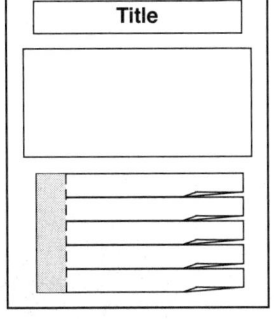

Demonstrate What You Have Learned

List the names of the major oceans of Earth in your science notebook. If you need help, use your science book or online sources.

Ocean Water

Major Ocean Zones

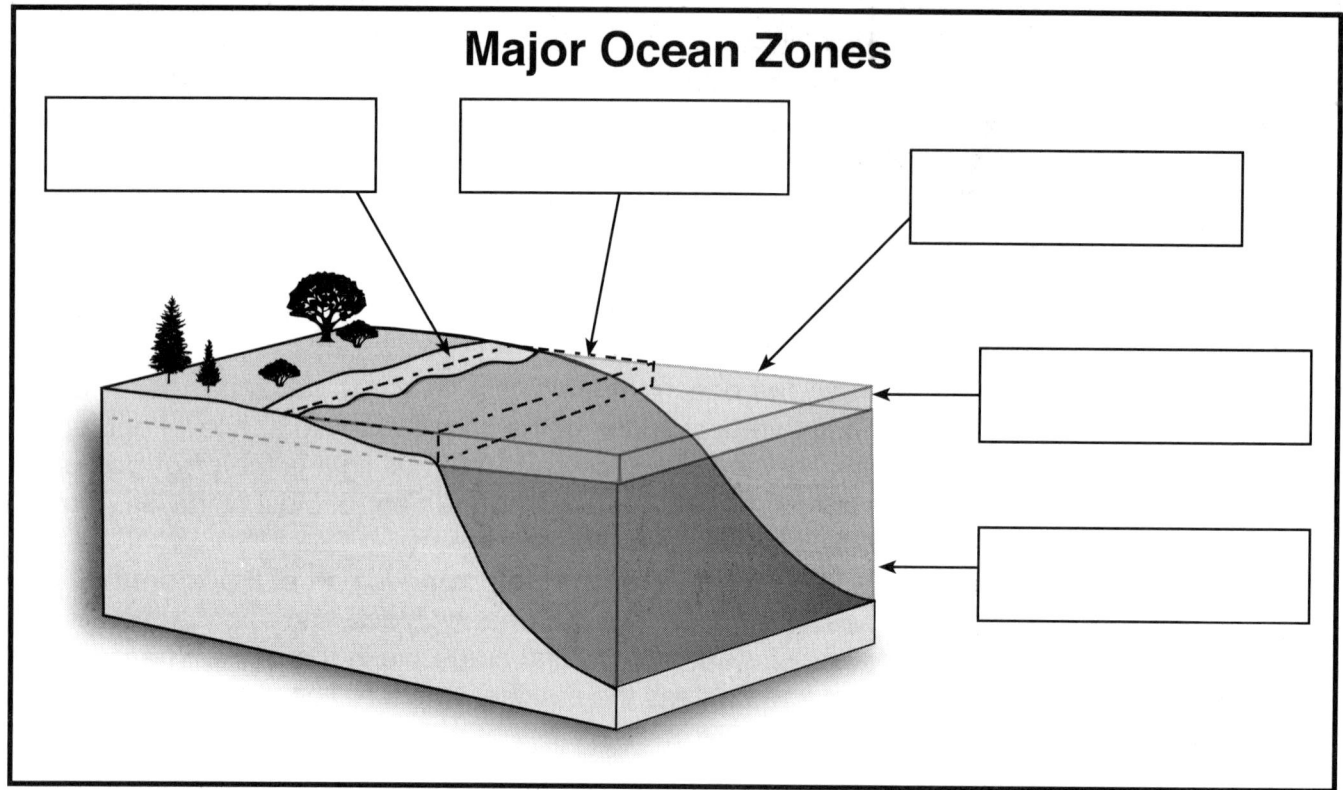

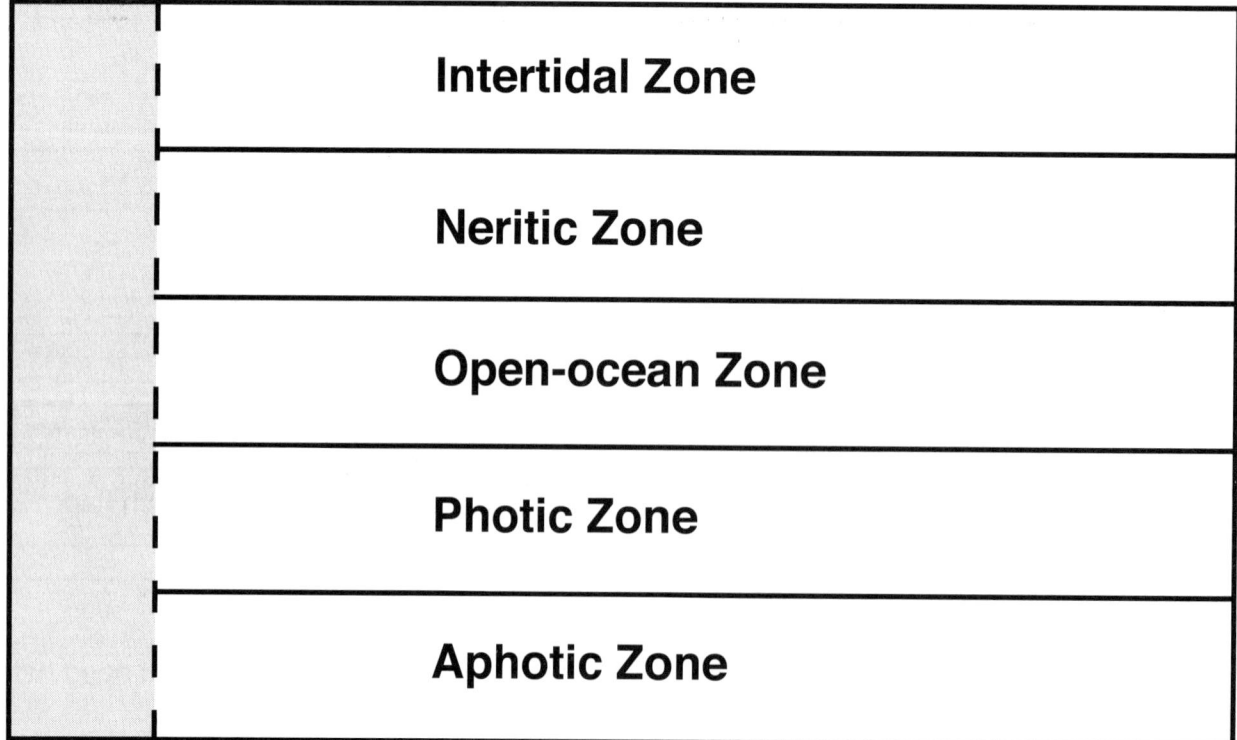

Intertidal Zone

Neritic Zone

Open-ocean Zone

Photic Zone

Aphotic Zone

Ocean Currents

Mini-Lesson

Read the following information. Then cut out and attach this box to the right-hand page of your science notebook. Use what you have learned to create the left-hand page.

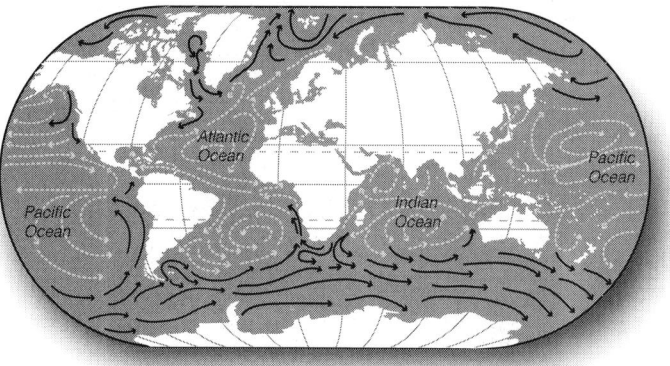

Light arrows are warm currents.
Dark arrows are cold currents.

Water density changes with both temperature and salinity. This causes motion beneath the waves called **currents**, which are essentially rivers of water that flow through oceans. The temperature of ocean currents directly affects the temperature of the air above them. In general, warm ocean currents flow away from the equator, and cool currents flow toward the equator.

Wind drives the ocean currents as Earth rotates on its axis (Coriolis Effect). This motion causes the ocean currents to move in a circular pattern. The currents move clockwise in the northern hemisphere and counterclockwise in the southern hemisphere.

Two Types of Ocean Currents
- **Surface currents** are the result of wind blowing over the ocean's surface. They are found in the upper 1,300 feet of water. There are two types of surface currents: cold and warm. Cold currents move from the polar regions toward the equator. Warm currents move from the tropical latitudes toward the poles. Waves that crash into the shoreline are caused by surface currents. These waves cause beach erosion.
- **Subsurface currents** are rivers of cold salty water that flow deep in the ocean. They are found below 1,300 feet in the ocean. They are the result of denser, cold, salty water sinking below the less dense, warm, and less salty water of the surface currents. These currents transport nutrients that are used by the plants and animals that live in the ocean.

How to Create Your Left-Hand Notebook Page

Complete the following steps to create the left-hand page of your science notebook. Use lots of color.

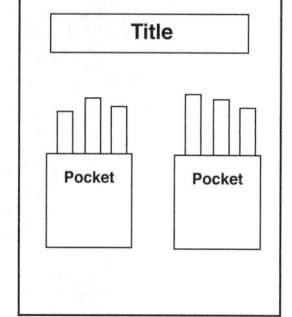

Step 1: Cut out the title and glue it to the top of the notebook page.
Step 2: Cut out the two pockets. Fold back the gray tabs on the dotted lines. Apply glue to the tabs and attach the pockets below the title.
Step 3: Cut apart the word strips. Place each strip in the correct pocket.

Demonstrate What You Have Learned

Go online to <www.youtube.com/watch?v=i2mec3vgeal> to view a video about the Coriolis Effect.

Ocean Currents

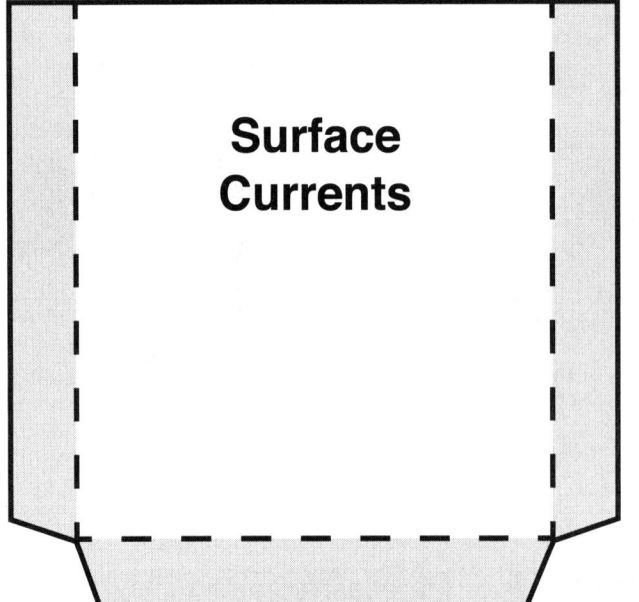

found below 1,300 ft. in the ocean
result of wind blowing over the ocean's surface
result of denser, cold, salty water sinking below the less dense, warm, and less salty water
found in the upper 1,300 ft. of ocean water
causes beach erosion
transports nutrients

Interactive Notebook: Earth & Space Science　　Oceanography: Parts of the Ocean Floor—Mini-Lesson

Parts of the Ocean Floor

Mini-Lesson

Read the following information. Then cut out and attach this box to the right-hand page of your science notebook. Use what you have learned to create the left-hand page.

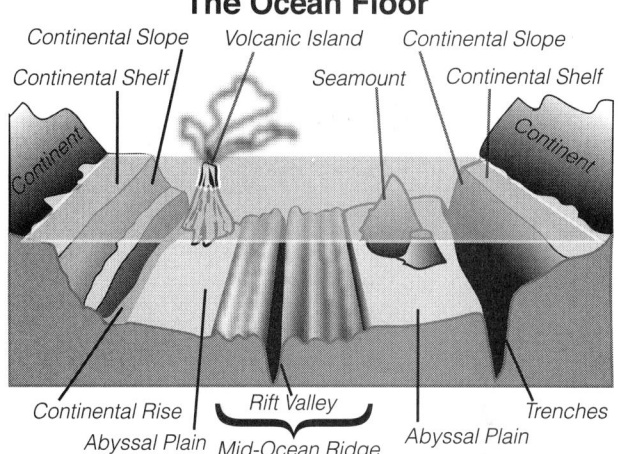

The continents do not end at the shoreline. They continue under the sea to the deep ocean floor. Many of the ocean floor features have been discovered using sonar. Oceanographers send a beam of sound waves aimed at the ocean floor. The sound waves bounce back to a recorder that measures the time it took for the waves to travel from the ocean surface to the ocean floor and back.

The **continental shelf** is the land near the shoreline that is covered with water. At the end of the shelf, the land plunges downward sharply, forming the **continental slope**. At the bottom of the continental slope, sediment that drifted down from the continental shelf and slope forms the **continental rise**. At the bottom of the continental rise, the abyssal plain begins. The **abyssal plain** is a flat, sediment-covered area that covers a vast amount of the deep ocean floor.

Deep-sea trenches are the lowest places on Earth. Active volcanoes and earthquakes are common along trenches. **Rift zones** are regions where the seafloor is spreading apart; it is here that magma from Earth's interior seeps onto the seafloor through cracks formed by the gap between the plate boundaries. This includes the area of mid-ocean ridges and rift valleys. **Mid-ocean ridges** are long, continuous chains of underwater mountains that wind through Earth's oceans. The ridges form alongside rift zones. **Rift valleys** are lowland regions that form where Earth's tectonic plates move apart.

Seamounts are underwater mountains formed by volcanic activity. **Volcanic islands** are made from volcanoes erupting from the ocean floor.

How to Create Your Left-Hand Notebook Page

Complete the following steps to create the left-hand page of your science notebook. Use lots of color.

Step 1: Cut out the title and glue it to the top of the page.
Step 2: Cut out the diagram chart. Apply glue to the back and attach it below the title. Draw and label the parts of the ocean floor.
Step 3: Fill in the chart with the correct definitions.

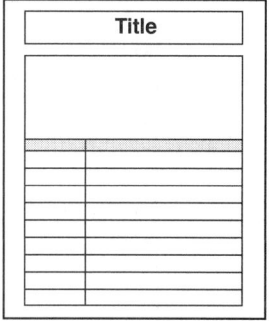

Demonstrate What You Have Learned

Create a 3-D model that represents the major features of the ocean floor. Use online sources to help you find a creative idea.

Parts of the Ocean Floor

Ocean Floor

Feature	Definition
continental shelf	
continental slope	
continental rise	
abyssal plain	
deep-sea trench	
mid-ocean ridge	
rift valley	
seamount	
volcanic island	

Interactive Notebook: Earth & Space Science Meteorology: Earth's Atmosphere—Mini-Lesson

Earth's Atmosphere

Mini-Lesson

Read the following information. Then cut out and attach this box to the right-hand page of your science notebook. Use what you have learned to create the left-hand page.

The **atmosphere** is the layer of air that surrounds the earth and extends from Earth's surface to outer space. It is made up of nitrogen, oxygen, water vapor, and other gases. Earth's atmosphere has been divided into five main layers: troposphere, stratosphere, mesosphere, thermosphere, and exosphere.

- The **troposphere** is the layer closest to the earth. All weather occurs in this layer. The troposphere extends from 0 km to 16 km (0 mi. to 9 mi.) above the earth. The temperature here decreases with altitude.
- The **stratosphere** is the layer above the troposphere extending from 16 km to 50 km (9 mi. to 31 mi.). Jet planes often fly in this layer because there are few clouds or weather events to bump them around. The ozone layer is at the top of the stratosphere, protecting us from harmful UV rays from the sun. The temperature in this layer increases with altitude. The formation of ozone causes heat, which increases from an average of -51°C (-60°F) at the tropopause to -15°C (5°F) at the top of the stratosphere. The tropopause is the boundary between the troposphere and the stratosphere.
- The **mesosphere** extends from 50 km to 90 km (31 mi. to 56 mi.). It is the coldest layer of the atmosphere at -90°C (-130°F). The mesosphere protects Earth from meteors or shooting stars; they burn up here. Radio waves are reflected from this layer back to Earth.
- The **thermosphere** extends from 90 km to 300 km (56 mi. to 186 mi.). It is the hottest layer of the atmosphere at 1,500°C (2,732°F). Astronauts orbiting Earth in the space station spend their time in this layer. Auroras, dancing curtains of light, can be seen in this layer.
- The **exosphere** is the outermost layer that extends from 300 km to 600 km (186 mi. to 373 mi.) then gradually fades into the vacuum of space. Artificial satellites orbit here where the temperature increases with altitude and ranges from 0°C to 1,700°C (32°F to 3,092°F).

How to Create Your Left-Hand Notebook Page

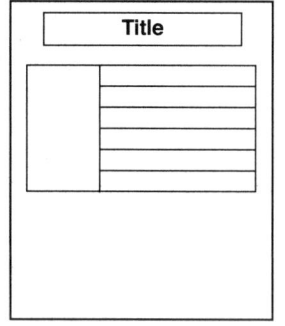

Complete the following steps to create the left-hand page of your science notebook. Use lots of color.

Step 1: Cut out the title and glue it to the top of the notebook page.
Step 2: Cut out the chart. Apply glue to the back and attach it below the title.
Step 3: Cut apart the word cards and glue each card in the correct box on the chart.

Demonstrate What You Have Learned

Create a model of the five layers of Earth's atmosphere that represents the characteristics of each layer. Use online sources to help you find a creative idea.

Earth's Atmosphere

EXOSPHERE	
THERMOSPHERE	
MESOSPHERE	
STRATOSPHERE	
TROPOSPHERE	
	The atmosphere is the layer of air that surrounds the earth and extends from Earth's surface to outer space.

This layer protects Earth from meteors or shooting stars.

All weather occurs in this layer.

Astronauts orbiting Earth in the space station spend their time in this layer.

Jet planes often fly in this layer because there are few clouds or weather events.

Artificial satellites orbit here.

The Water Cycle

Mini-Lesson

Read the following information. Then cut out and attach this box to the right-hand page of your science notebook. Use what you have learned to create the left-hand page.

The amount of water on the earth has remained the same since its formation. Much of the water is contained in oceans, lakes, ponds, and rivers. Water can also be contained in the ground in the form of groundwater. This water may be in the soil or hidden in underground aquifers. Water can also be contained in plants and animals.

Most of the water that comes to the ground from the atmosphere arrives in some form of precipitation, such as rain or snow. The water that lands on the earth's surface may be either absorbed into the ground and become part of the groundwater system or it might run into a lake, stream, pond, or some other body of water.

The **water cycle** describes how water continuously moves throughout the earth and its atmosphere in the repeated process of evaporation, transpiration, condensation, and precipitation.

- The earth's water enters the atmosphere through **evaporation**; heat from the sun causes water on Earth to turn from liquid to gas and rise into the sky. This water vapor collects in the sky in the form of clouds.
- **Transpiration** is the process whereby plants and animals release water vapor into the atmosphere. Animals release water vapor when they exhale moisture from their lungs, and plants through their leaves during the process of photosynthesis.
- **Condensation** is the movement of water from a gaseous state to a liquid state. During condensation, water vapor in the clouds cools down and becomes liquid again. Condensation is the basis by which clouds are formed, both in the sky and near the ground as fog.
- **Precipitation** occurs when water in liquid and solid form becomes so large and heavy it can no longer stay in the earth's atmosphere and water falls back to the earth in the form of rain, hail, sleet, snow, or mist.

How to Create Your Left-Hand Notebook Page

Complete the following steps to create the left-hand page of your science notebook. Use lots of color.

Step 1: Cut out the title and glue it to the top of the notebook page.
Step 2: Cut out the diagram box. Apply glue to the back and attach it below the title.
Step 3: Cut out the four word cards and glue each card in the correct box on the diagram.

Demonstrate What You Have Learned

Fill a small cup about one-half full of water. Add a drop of red food coloring to the water. Place the cup upright in one corner of a re-sealable plastic bag as you hold the opposite corner of the bag up. Seal the bag. Tape the bag upright in a location that receives daily sunlight. Observe the bag daily for a week and record any changes you observe in your science notebook.

The Water Cycle

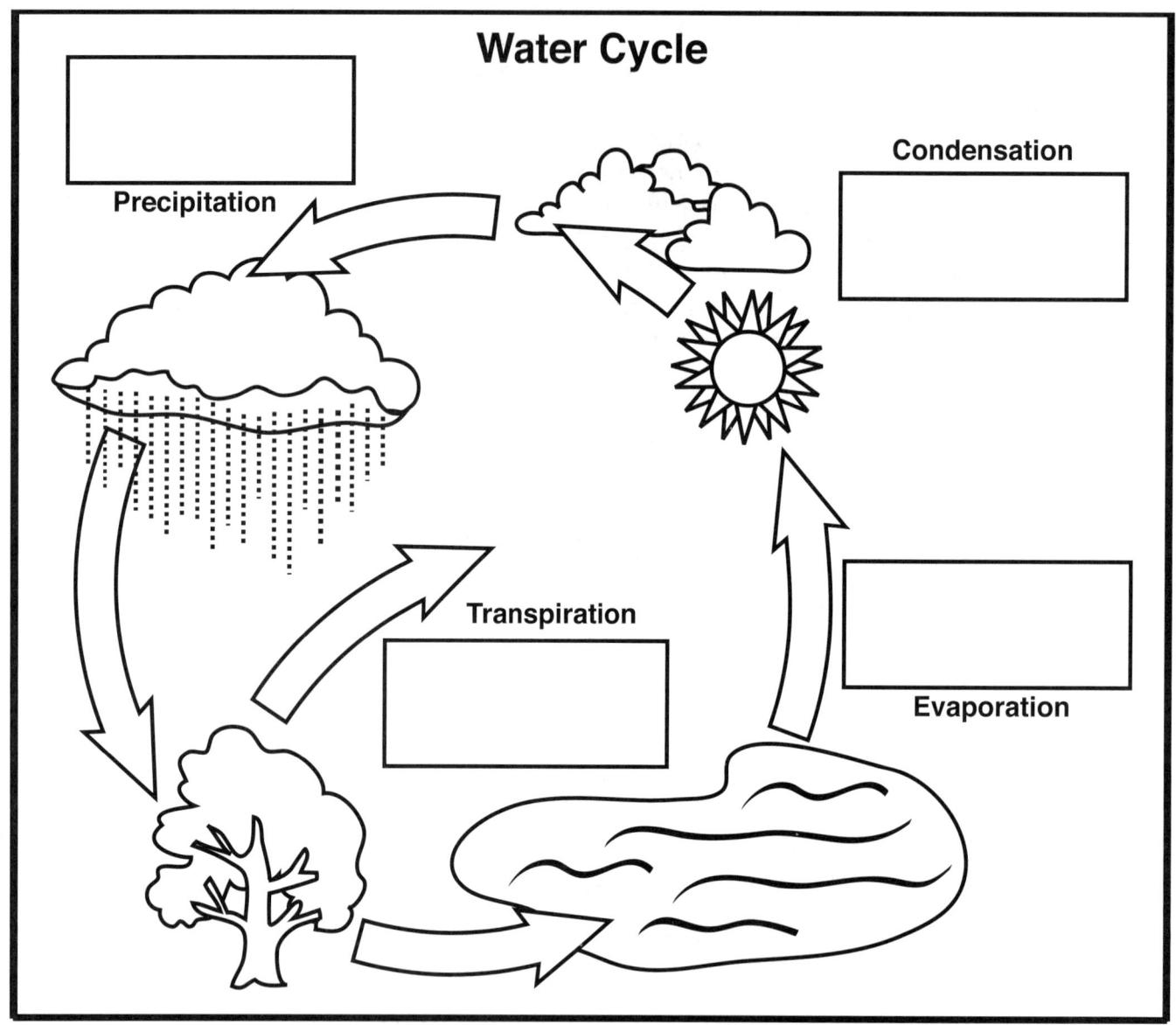

| plants and animals release water vapor into the atmosphere | water falls back to the earth in the form of rain, hail, sleet, snow, or mist |

| movement of water from a gaseous state to a liquid state | heat from the sun causes water to turn from liquid to gas and rise into the sky |

Factors Affecting Climate

Mini-Lesson

Read the following information. Then cut out and attach this box to the right-hand page of your science notebook. Use what you have learned to create the left-hand page.

Weather for a particular area over a long period of time is called **climate**. Climate includes seasonal changes in weather. Several factors lead to a rich variety of climates.

Temperature
- **Latitude** is the distance of a place north or south of the equator. Temperatures are generally lower as you get farther from the equator.
- **Elevation** (altitude) is the distance of an area above sea level. Air thins as you climb a mountain; thin air holds less heat. Therefore, temperatures usually decrease as elevation increases.
- **Ocean currents** directly affect the temperature of the air above them. In general, warm ocean currents flow away from the equator, and cool currents flow toward the equator. Major currents like the Gulf Stream can significantly warm the air near landmasses that would otherwise be quite cold.

Precipitation
- **Prevailing winds** are winds that blow more often from one direction than the other. They may be warm or cold and carry varying amounts of water, depending on whether they are blowing off water or land.
- **Mountain ranges** alter the flow of prevailing winds. Air must rise to get over a mountain, and rising air cools and becomes incapable of holding as much water. Therefore, the side of a mountain facing the prevailing wind (the windward side) tends to get a lot of moisture. The leeward side of the same mountain gets sinking air stripped of most of its moisture, often resulting in a desert in the mountain's so-called "rain shadow."

How to Create Your Left-Hand Notebook Page

Complete the following steps to create the left-hand page of your science notebook. Use lots of color.

Step 1: Cut out the title and glue it to the top of the notebook page.
Step 2: Cut out the flap chart. Cut on the solid lines to create five vocabulary flaps. Apply glue to the back of the gray tab and attach the chart below the title.
Step 3: Write the correct definition under each flap.

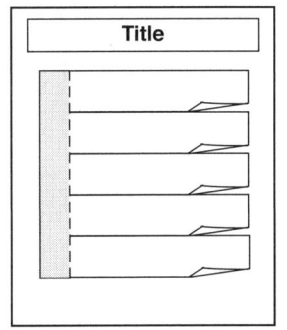

Demonstrate What You Have Learned

Research the three major climate zones on earth: polar, tropical, and temperate. Describe each climate zone including the location, temperature, and seasons in your science notebook.

Factors Affecting Climate

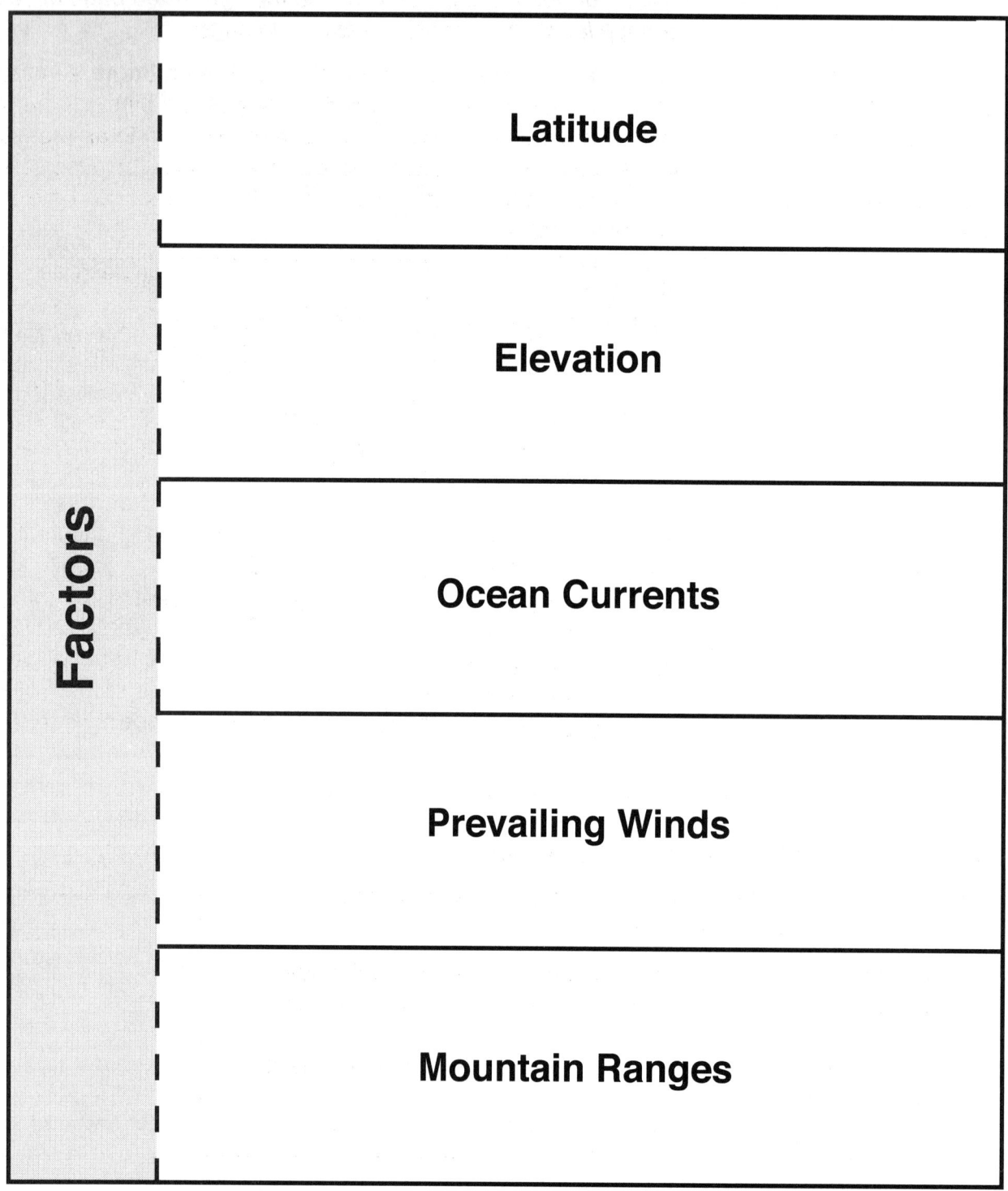

Factors:
- Latitude
- Elevation
- Ocean Currents
- Prevailing Winds
- Mountain Ranges

Air Masses

Mini-Lesson

Read the following information. Then cut out and attach this box to the right-hand page of your science notebook. Use what you have learned to create the left-hand page.

Weather is the condition of the air at a given place and time on the earth. An air mass is a large body of air with consistent temperature and humidity that passes over the earth. Movements of air masses are used to forecast the weather. Meteorologists define air masses by where they form. **Maritime air masses** assemble over oceans and are made up of moist air. **Continental air masses** build over land and are made up of dry air. North America contends with four types of air masses that affect weather.

- **Maritime tropical (mT)** air masses form over the warm waters of the Gulf of Mexico. The moist air moves northward into the United States, increasing the possibility of precipitation.
- **Maritime polar (mP)** air masses form over the northern Pacific and Atlantic Oceans. They carry cool, moist air into the United States.
- **Continental tropical (cT)** air masses occur in the summer and form over Mexico. They bring hot air to the southwestern states.
- **Continental polar (cP)** air masses form over northern Canada and may cause the mercury in thermometers in northern states to nosedive. The air is cold and contains little moisture.

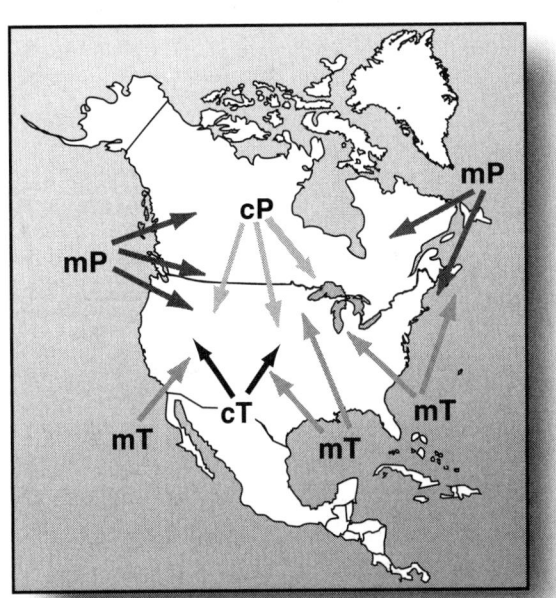

How to Create Your Left-Hand Notebook Page

Complete the following steps to create the left-hand page of your science notebook. Use lots of color.

Step 1: Cut out the title and glue it to the top of the notebook page.
Step 2: Cut out the diagram box. Apply glue to the back and attach it below the title.
Step 3: Cut out the six word cards and glue each card in the correct oval on the diagram.

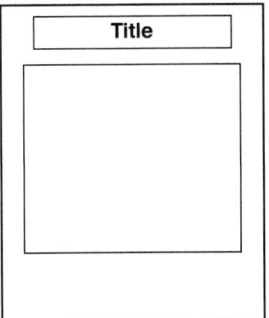

Demonstrate What You Have Learned

Watch the national weather forecast during a one-week time period. Record the impact of air masses on the weather across the country in your science notebook.

Air Masses

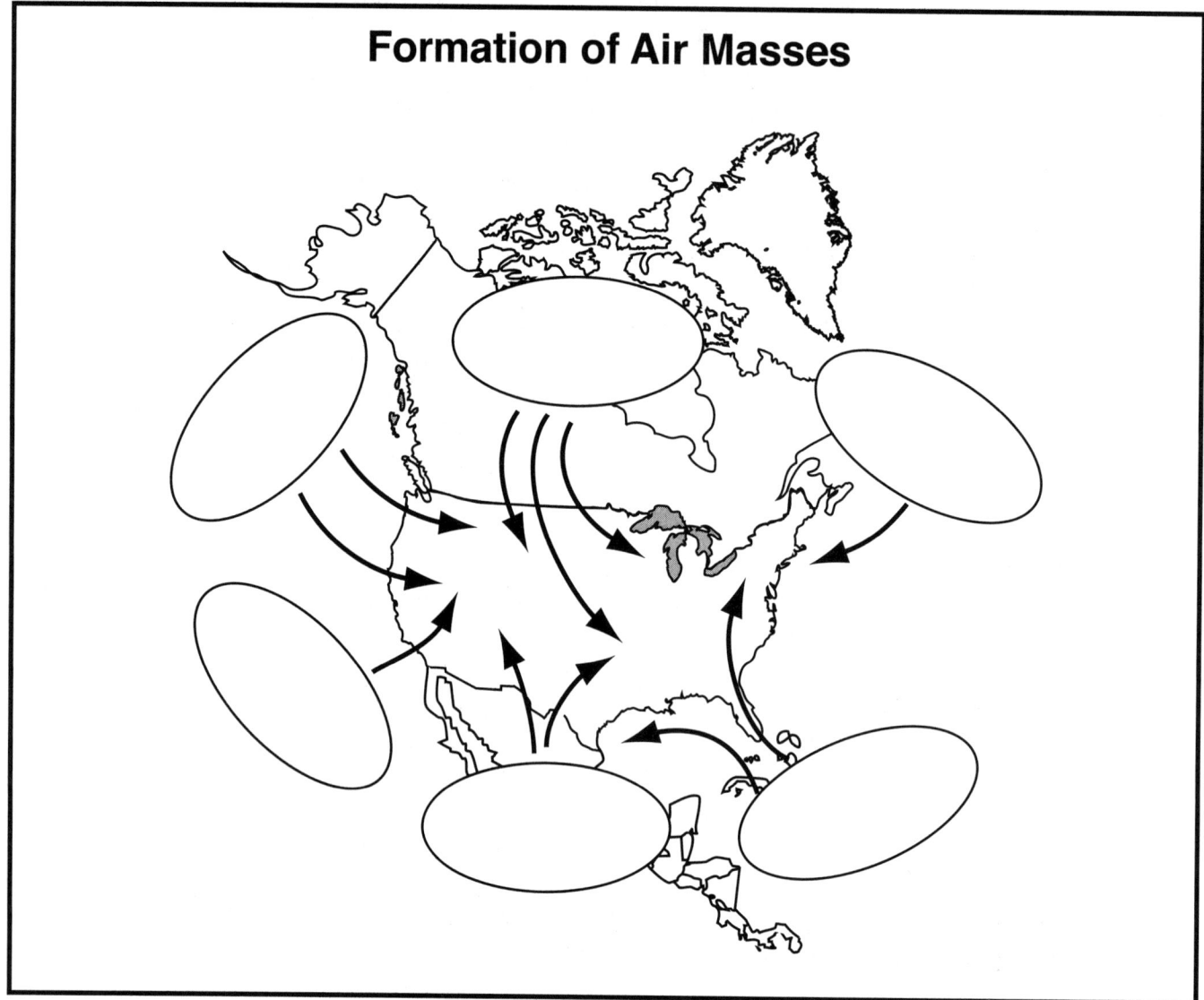

Formation of Air Masses

- Maritime Polar
- Continental Tropical
- Maritime Tropical
- Maritime Polar
- Continental Polar
- Maritime Tropical

Cold and Warm Fronts

Mini-Lesson

Read the following information. Then cut out and attach this box to the right-hand page of your science notebook. Use what you have learned to create the left-hand page.

Points of contact between air masses are called **fronts**. Fronts are found along leading edges of air masses. The temperature and pressure of the advancing air mass dictates the name of the front. Fronts are where active weather occurs. Most weather systems move from the west-southwest to east-northeast. Meteorologists use symbols to represent fronts on a weather map.

Four Types of Fronts

- A **cold front** forms when a cold air mass overtakes a warm air mass. Typically, cold, dense air plows under warm, moist air, causing it to rise rapidly. Such a front is likely to bring violent storms with heavy rain showers as the warm, moist air is quickly cooled when it rises. Storms are followed by fair, cooler weather.

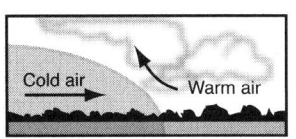

- A **warm front** forms when a warm air mass overtakes a cold air mass. The less dense, warm air tends to slide over the heavy, dense cooled air. Stratus clouds often occur along with longer periods of steady rainfall. Rainfall is followed by warmer, more humid weather.

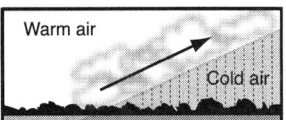

- A **stationary front** occurs when air masses tend to remain in place for a period of time. This type of front often brings many days of almost continuous precipitation.

- An **occluded front** forms when two cold air masses collide and push a warm air mass up between them. This type of front usually brings light rain or other precipitation.

How to Create Your Left-Hand Notebook Page

Complete the following steps to create the left-hand page of your science notebook. Use lots of color.

Step 1: Cut out the title and glue it to the top of the notebook page.
Step 2: Cut out the chart. Apply glue to back and attach it below the title.
Step 3: Cut out the four word cards and glue each card in the correct box on the chart.
Step 4: Write the type of weather each front brings in the correct box on the chart.

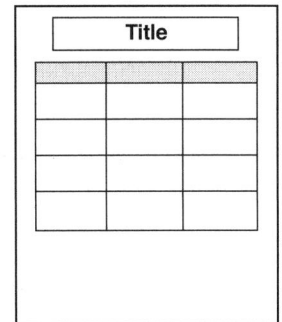

Demonstrate What You Have Learned

Watch the national weather forecast for three days. Record the formation and movement of fronts in your science notebook. Based on your observation and collected data, write a weather forecast for the next day.

Cold and Warm Fronts

Type of Front and Symbol	How Front Forms	Weather Front Brings
Cold Front ▲▲▲		
Warm Front ⌒⌒⌒		
Stationary Front ▲⌒▲⌒		
Occluded Front ▲⌒▲⌒		

two cold air masses collide and push a warm air mass up between them

air masses tend to remain in place for a period of time

a cold air mass overtakes a warm air mass

a warm air mass overtakes a cold air mass

Clouds and Precipitation

Mini-Lesson

Read the following information. Then cut out and attach this box to the right-hand page of your science notebook. Use what you have learned to create the left-hand page.

Clouds are a collection of millions of tiny water droplets or ice crystals suspended in the troposphere layer of the atmosphere. In order for clouds to form, three ingredients are necessary: water vapor, condensation nuclei, and cooling. As water vapor cools, it reaches saturation point and condenses around **condensation nuclei**, tiny particles such as dust and smoke within the atmosphere. Condensed water appears as tiny **cloud droplets**. Large groups of tiny water drops appear as clouds. Depending upon the temperature, the tiny water droplets may freeze or remain in a liquid state. That is why most high-level clouds are tiny particles of ice, even though they appear to be white. Closer to the earth, water vapor condenses on a surface and can be observed in the form of **dew** on the grass or as **frost**, if the temperature is below freezing. Clouds are classified by their shape and altitude in the atmosphere. Stratus, cumulus, and cirrus are the three main cloud types.

Stratus clouds form at low altitudes. They form layers of sheet-like clouds and are associated with steady rains, snow, or very cloudy days. Stratus clouds at ground level are called **fog**. **Nimbostratus clouds** are dark stratus clouds that usually produce light to heavy continuous rain.

Cumulus clouds usually form at mid-altitude. These are flat bottom, fluffy clouds associated with fair weather. **Cumulonimbus clouds** are a type of cumulus clouds. They are tall, dark, and very fluffy. They are often called thunder clouds. They may produce rain, hail, lightening, thunder, and tornadoes.

Cirrus clouds form at high altitudes; they are long and feathery and made of ice crystals. They are often seen before a weather change such as rain or snow.

Precipitation occurs when water droplets in liquid and solid form become so large and heavy they can no longer be held by the clouds. The most common forms of precipitation include rain and snow. Perhaps less common forms include sleet, freezing rain, and hail.

How to Create Your Left-Hand Notebook Page

Complete the following steps to create the left-hand page of your science notebook. Use lots of color.

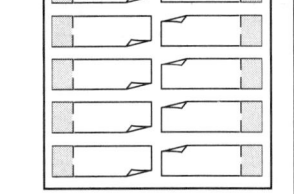

Step 1: Cut out the title and glue it to the top of the notebook page.
Step 2: Cut out the puzzle flaps. Match each vocabulary word with the correct example. Apply glue to the back of each gray tab and attach the flaps below the title.
Step 3: Write the type of weather produced by each cloud formation under the correct flap.

Demonstrate What You Have Learned *(Teacher supervision required.)*

Pour 20 mL of cold water in a 2-liter plastic bottle. Swirl the water around the bottle. Strike a match. Drop the match into the plastic bottle. Cap the plastic bottle. Squeeze the bottle and then let go. Repeat the activity using warm water. In your science notebook, compare the difference in cloud formation.

Clouds and Precipitation

Stratus Clouds

tall, dark, and very fluffy clouds

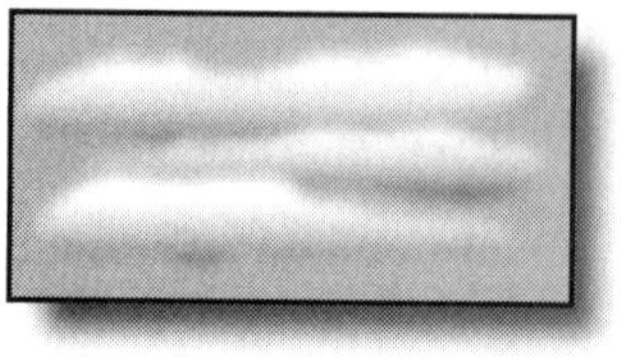

Nimbostratus Clouds

layers of sheet-like clouds

Cumulus Clouds

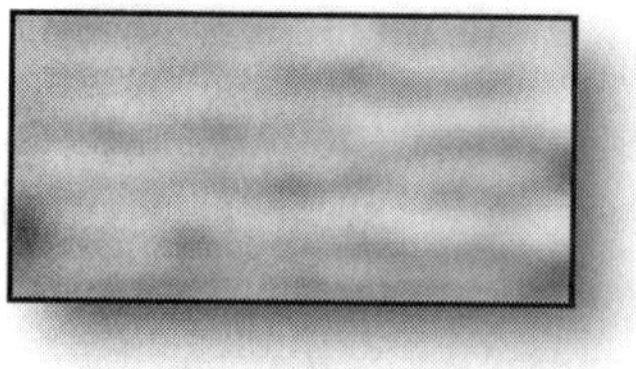

dark layers of sheet-like clouds

Cumulonimbus Clouds

long and feathery clouds

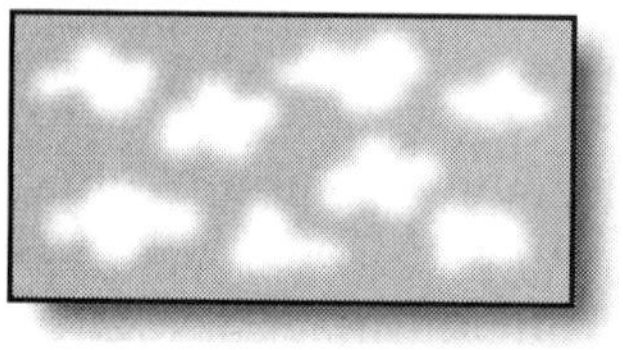

Cirrus Clouds

flat bottom, fluffy clouds

Air Pressure and Wind

Mini-Lesson

Read the following information. Then cut out and attach this box to the right-hand page of your science notebook. Use what you have learned to create the left-hand page.

Air pressure, also called barometric pressure, is a measure of the weight of air pressing down on the surface of the earth. Meteorologists use changes in air pressure to help predict the weather for a given area. Falling air pressure means that stormy weather is on its way. Rising air pressure means fair weather is on its way. If air pressure remains steady, the weather an area is having is likely to continue. Meteorologists use an instrument called a **barometer** to measure change in air pressure.

Wind, or moving air, is caused by the differences in air pressure. Air moves from areas of high pressure to areas of low pressure. Winds blow in a counterclockwise direction in regions of rising warm moist air and are called **low pressure systems**. Clouds, rain, or snow and strong winds often occur in these regions. Heavy cooler air blows to where the warmer, lighter air was. Winds blow in a clockwise direction in regions of sinking cool air and are called **high pressure systems**. Meteorologists use an instrument called an **anemometer** to measure wind speed. A **wind vane**, sometimes called a weather vane, is used to determine wind direction, or the direction from which wind blows.

Local winds blow over small areas. **Global winds** are a system of wind patterns caused by the spinning of Earth, referred to as the **Coriolis effect**, and the differences in temperature between the equator and the polar areas. There are three different global wind patterns.

- **Trade winds:** warm, steady winds that blow back toward the equator from the northeast in the Northern Hemisphere and from the southeast in the Southern Hemisphere.
- **Prevailing westerlies:** air that usually moves quickly toward the poles from west to east in both hemispheres.
- **Polar easterlies:** cold, fairly weak winds from the poles blowing from east to west.

How to Create Your Left-Hand Notebook Page

Complete the following steps to create the left-hand page of your science notebook. Use lots of color.

Step 1: Cut out the title and glue it to the top of the notebook page.
Step 2: Cut out the diagram chart. Apply glue to the back and attach it below the title. Correctly label the global wind patterns.
Step 3: Cut out the four word cards and glue each card in the correct box on the chart.

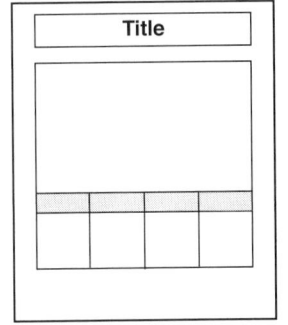

Demonstrate What You Have Learned

Research how to make a homemade barometer. Follow the directions to construct your own weather instrument. Read your barometer at the same time each day for several days and record the data in your science notebook.

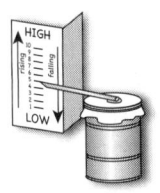

Air Pressure and Wind

Global Wind Patterns

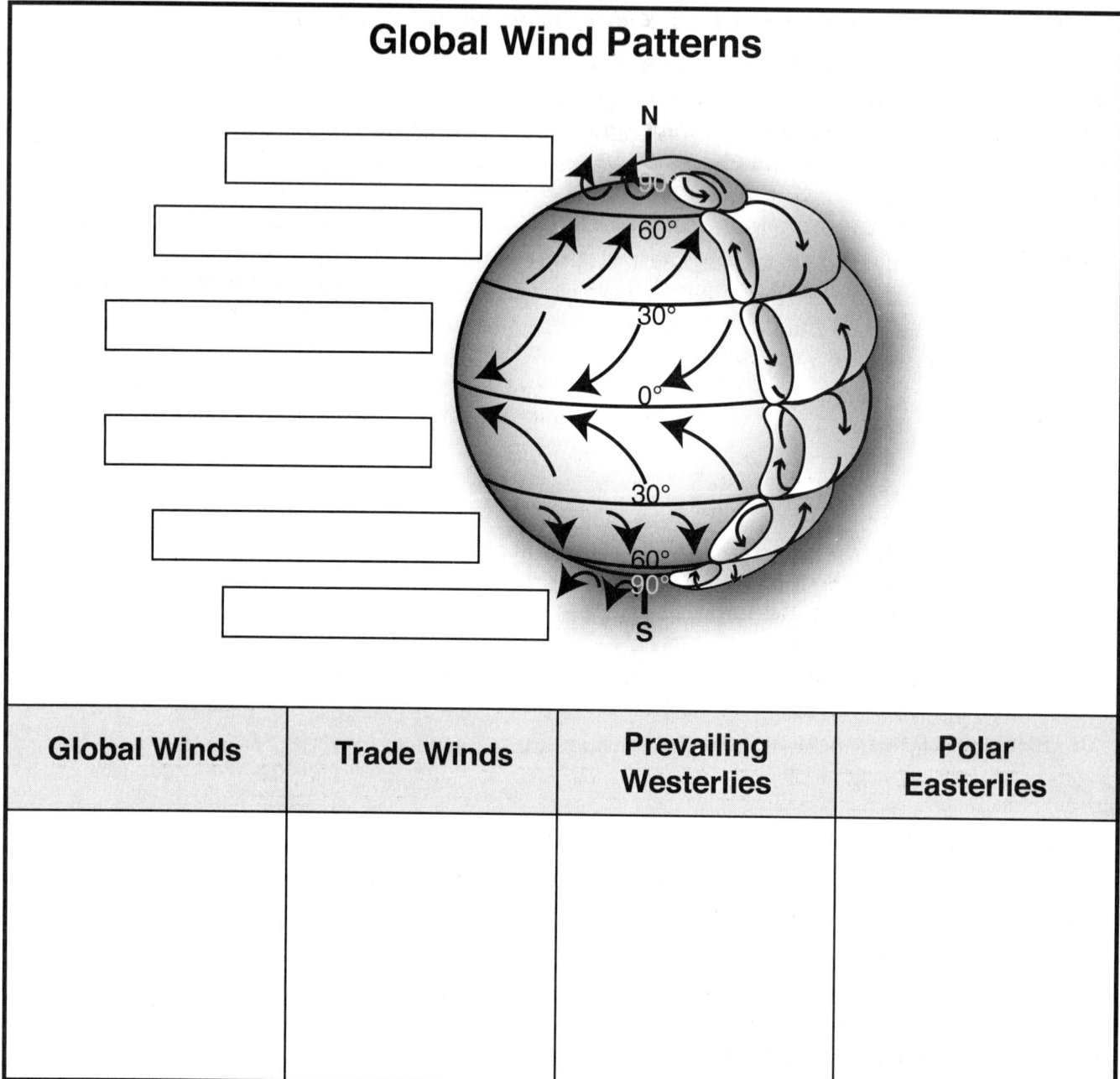

Global Winds	Trade Winds	Prevailing Westerlies	Polar Easterlies

air moving toward the poles from west to east in both hemispheres	winds from the poles blowing from east to west	a system of wind patterns	winds blowing back toward the equator

Humidity and Dew Point

Mini-Lesson

Read the following information. Then cut out and attach this box to the right-hand page of your science notebook. Use what you have learned to create the left-hand page.

Water on Earth enters the atmosphere through **evaporation**. Heat from the sun causes water on Earth to turn from liquid to gas (**water vapor**) and rise into the sky. Water vapor molecules take up space among the air molecules. Air at different temperatures is capable of holding varying amounts of moisture. Warm air holds more water molecules than cold air. **Humidity** is a measure of the amount of moisture or water vapor in the air.

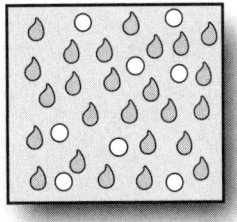 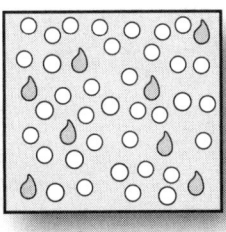

Warm Air   Cool Air

Water vapor molecules are shown as drops, and air molecules are shown as circles.

Relative humidity (reported as a percentage) is defined as the amount of moisture in the air relative to what it could hold if the air were entirely saturated at a given temperature. Air saturated with water vapor has a relative humidity of 100%. When humidity is high, rain clouds or fog are more likely to form. A **hygrometer** is an instrument meteorologists use for measuring relative humidity. A **psychrometer** is a type of hygrometer. A psychrometer consists of two thermometers, one of which includes a dry bulb and the other of which includes a bulb that is kept wet. The difference in the two thermometer readings is used to determine humidity.

In order for clouds to form, the water vapor in the air must condense and become liquid again. The temperature at which condensation occurs is known as the **dew point**. The dew point changes with the amount of water vapor in the air. Closer to the earth, water vapor condenses on a surface and can be observed in the form of **dew** on the grass or **frost**, if the temperature is below freezing.

How to Create Your Left-Hand Notebook Page

Complete the following steps to create the left-hand page of your science notebook. Use lots of color.

Step 1: Cut out the title and glue it to the top of the notebook page.
Step 2: Cut out the three flap charts. Apply glue to the back of each gray tab and attach the charts below the title.
Step 3: Write the correct definition under each flap.

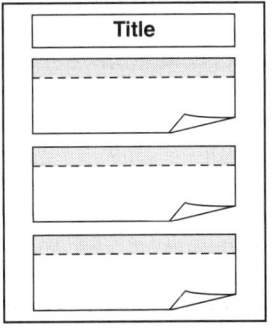

Demonstrate What You Have Learned

Find the dew point of the air in your classroom. Fill a metal can approximately one-third full of room temperature water. Slowly add ice to the water and stir. Add more ice as the ice in the can melts. Observe the can until a thin film of moisture forms on the outside of the can. Measure and record the temperature of the water in the can, and record it in your science notebook. This is the dew point.

Humidity and Dew Point

Humidity

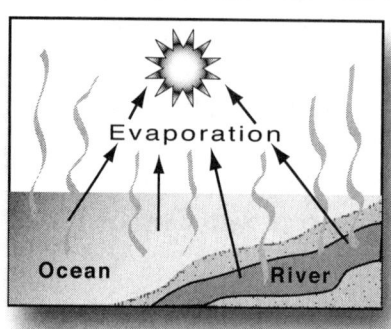

Hygrometer

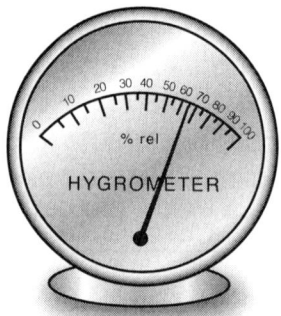

Dew Point

Our Solar System

Mini-Lesson

Read the following information. Then cut out and attach this box to the right-hand page of your science notebook. Use what you have learned to create the left-hand page.

Our **solar system** consists of a sun, planets, moons around the planets, asteroids, meteoroids, and comets. The solar system also includes solar wind and dust; however, most of the solar system is simply empty space. All the parts of the solar system move around other objects. The moons move around their planets. The planets move around the sun. The sun also moves around the center of the Milky Way Galaxy.

The sun is at the center of our solar system. The other members surround the sun and revolve around it, each in its own orbit. Astronomers believe that the sun is actually NOT directly in the center, but is slightly to one side. Most of the members of the system orbit the sun in **elliptical**, or oval, paths—not round ones. Their paths resemble the shape of an egg or a football.

The position of the planets in the solar system causes them to have unique physical features. The first four planets in the solar system are Mercury, Venus, Earth, and Mars. These planets are referred to as the inner belt, or **terrestrial planets**. The region between the inner planets and the outer planets is referred to as the **asteroid belt**. This is an area occupied by numerous asteroids traveling around the sun. The five planets in the outer belt of our solar system are Jupiter, Saturn, Uranus, Neptune, and Pluto. These planets are referred to as the **Jovian planets**. Jupiter, Saturn, Uranus, and Neptune are different from all the other planets in that they have no solid surface. These large gas giants are surrounded by gaseous clouds that get thicker closer to the center of the planet. Pluto is a cold, dense planet about which little is known. Pluto was once considered the most distant Jovian planet in our solar system. In 2006, because of its small size and eccentric orbit, the International Astronomical Union (IAU) formally reclassified it as a **dwarf planet**.

How to Create Your Left-Hand Notebook Page

Complete the following steps to create the left-hand page of your science notebook. Use lots of color.

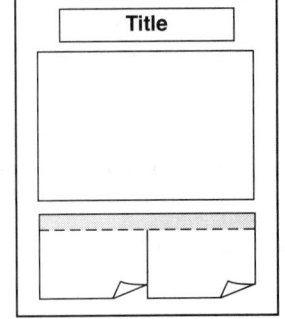

Step 1: Cut out the title and glue it to the top of the page.
Step 2: Cut out the diagram box. Apply glue to the back and attach it below the title. Label the diagram with the names of the planets.
Step 3: Cut out the flap chart. Cut on the solid line to create two flaps. Apply glue to the back of the gray tab and attach the chart at the bottom of the page. Write the names of the planets in the correct box on the chart. Write the correct definition under each flap.

Demonstrate What You Have Learned

Research each of the planets in our solar system. Find the following information for each planet: average distance from the sun, diameter, length of rotation, length of orbit, number of moons, and number of rings. Create a chart in your science notebook to record the information.

Interactive Notebook: Earth & Space Science   Astronomy: Our Solar System—Left-Hand Page

Our Solar System

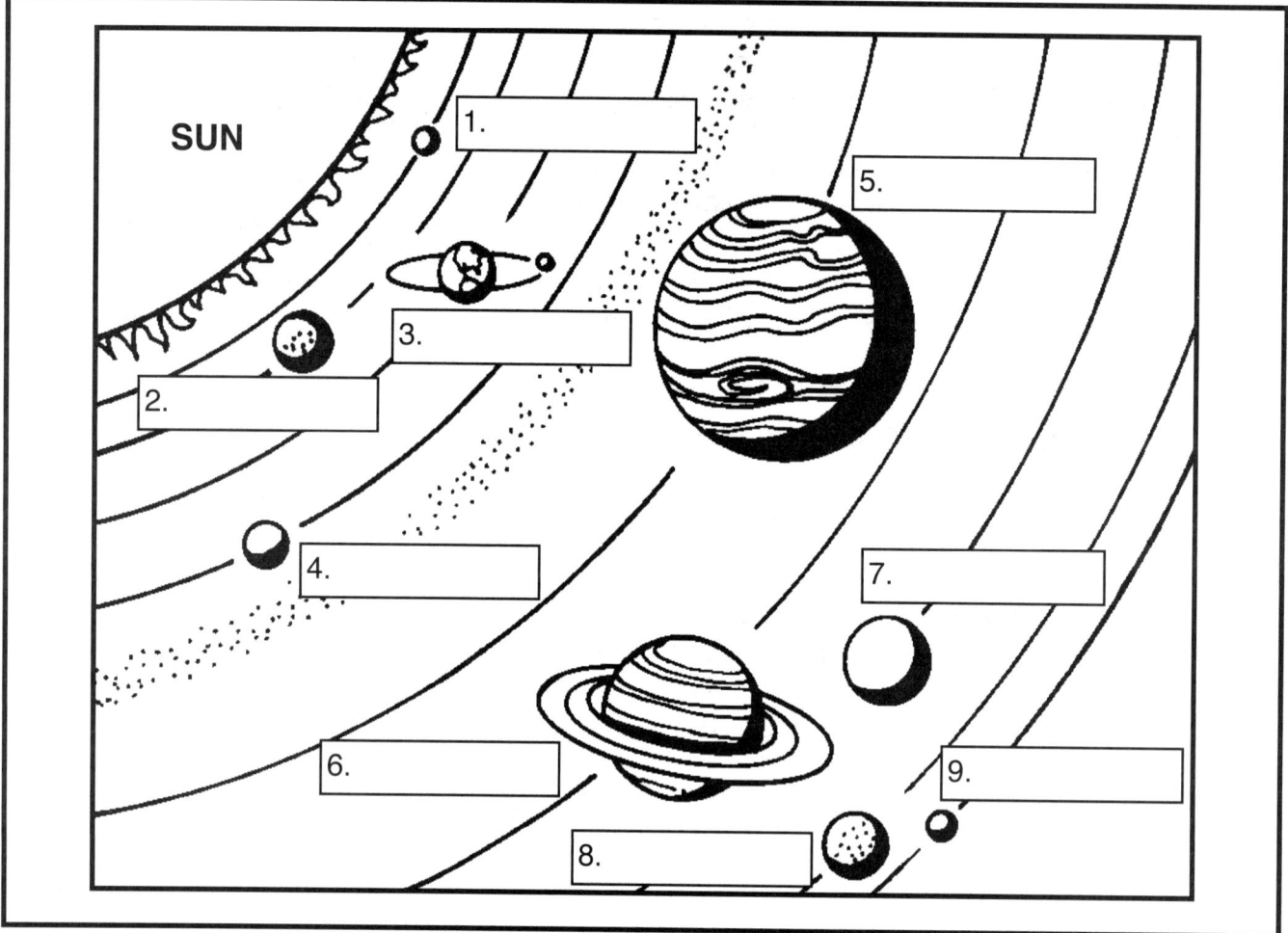

Terrestrial Planets	Jovian Planets

The Sun

Mini-Lesson

Read the following information. Then cut out and attach this box to the right-hand page of your science notebook. Use what you have learned to create the left-hand page.

The **sun** is the star found at the center of our solar system. It is a giant ball of burning hot gases, 15 million degrees Celsius at its core! Its interior and atmosphere are made up of several different layers.

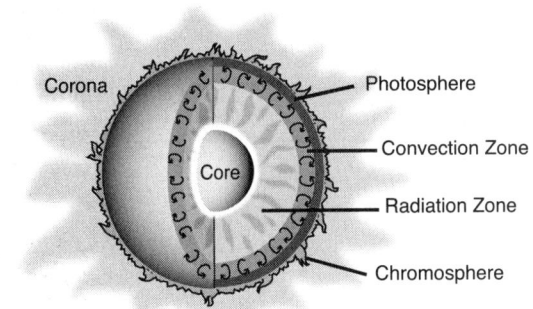

- The center of the sun is the **core**. It is a blazing furnace where hydrogen is constantly being converted into helium.
- The **radiation zone** is the thickest of the sun's layers. Here energy is transferred from atom to atom by the process of radiation until the gas enters the next layer.
- The **convection zone** is the outermost layer of the sun's interior. The hot gases entering this zone from the radiation zone rise rapidly toward the surface. As they rise, the gases begin to cool. They then fall back toward the bottom of this zone. The cycle of heating, rising, cooling, and falling is repeated over and over before the gas can finally reach the surface of the sun.
- The **photosphere** is the bright, shiny disk of the sun that we can see from Earth. Most of the light that actually reaches Earth comes from this layer.
- The **chromosphere** is the layer that appears bright red in color, but it can only be seen from Earth during a total solar eclipse. Normally, its light is blocked by the much brighter photosphere.
- The outermost layer of the sun's atmosphere is called the **corona**. This region is only visible during a total solar eclipse or with an instrument called a **coronagraph**.

How to Create Your Left-Hand Notebook Page

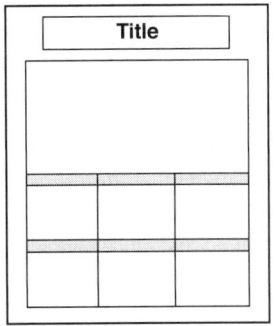

Complete the following steps to create the left-hand page of your science notebook. Use lots of color.

Step 1: Cut out the title and glue it to the top of the notebook page.
Step 2: Cut out the diagram chart. Apply glue to the back and attach it below the title. Label each part of the diagram.
Step 3: Write the correct definition in each box on the chart.

Demonstrate What You Have Learned

Research the sun. Use the information to create a list in your science notebook of safety tips for observing the sun.

The Sun

Layers of the Sun

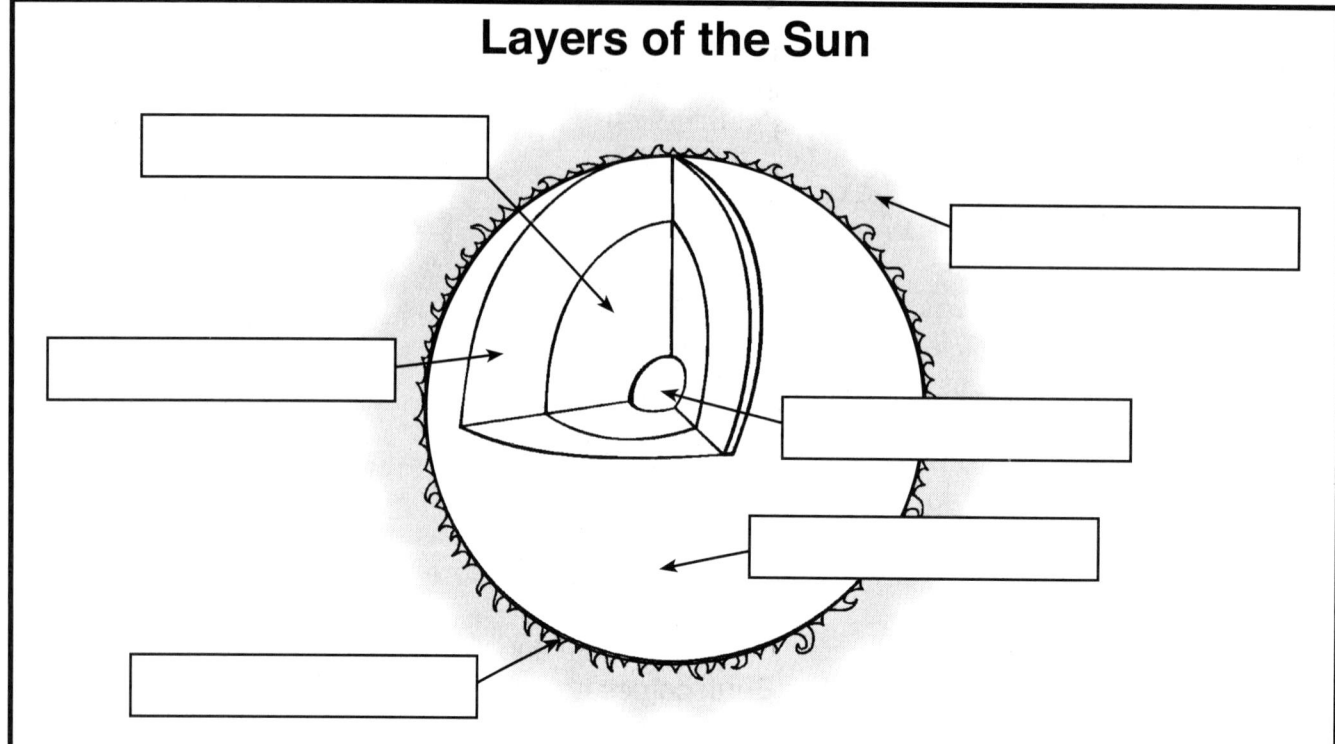

Core	Radiation Zone	Convection Zone

Photosphere	Chromosphere	Corona

Interactive Notebook: Earth & Space Science   Astronomy: Day and Night and the Seasons—Mini-Lesson

Day and Night and the Seasons

Mini-Lesson

Read the following information. Then cut out and attach this box to the right-hand page of your science notebook. Use what you have learned to create the left-hand page.

The earth is always spinning. As the earth moves, new parts of it come into the sun's light. This spinning motion of the earth is called **rotation**. It takes 23 hours and 26 minutes to complete one rotation. This makes one day on Earth. The earth rotates around its axis. The **axis** is an imaginary line that goes from the top of the earth, through the center, to the bottom of the earth. This rotation from west to east causes the sun to appear to move across the sky from east to west.

We owe our **seasons**—spring, summer, fall, and winter—to the **revolution** of the earth around the sun and to the 23.5 degrees tilt of Earth's axis. The earth makes a complete revolution around the sun every 365 and one-fourth days. This makes one year on Earth.

- The **summer solstice** marks the beginning of summer, and it is the longest day of the year. It occurs on or around June 21 in the Northern Hemisphere. On this day, Earth's North Pole is tilted toward the sun, and the Northern Hemisphere is as close to the sun as it can be. While the Northern Hemisphere is having summer, the people in the Southern Hemisphere are experiencing winter.
- The **winter solstice** marks the beginning of winter, and it's also the shortest day of the year. It occurs on or around December 21 in the Northern Hemisphere. On this day, Earth's North Pole is tilted away from the sun, and the Northern Hemisphere is as far from the sun as it can be. Therefore, the first day of winter has the least amount of sunlight. While the Northern Hemisphere is having winter, the people in the Southern Hemisphere are experiencing summer.
- The **spring equinox** marks the beginning of spring. It occurs on or around March 21 in the Northern Hemisphere when the sun crosses the area of the earth's equator, making night and day approximately equal in length all over the earth.
- The **autumnal equinox** marks the beginning of autumn. It occurs on or around September 22 in the Northern Hemisphere when the sun crosses the area of the earth's equator, making night and day approximately equal in length all over the earth.

How to Create Your Left-Hand Notebook Page

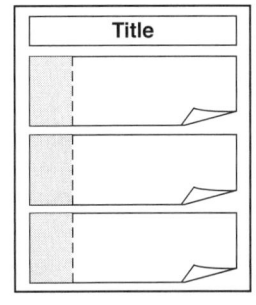

Complete the following steps to create the left-hand page of your science notebook. Use lots of color.

Step 1: Cut out the title and glue it to the top of the notebook page.

Step 2: Cut out the three flap charts. Apply glue to the back of each gray tab and attach the charts below the title. Write the correct explanation under each flap.

Demonstrate What You Have Learned

Research how time can be measured by following the regular pattern of shadows cast by the sun. Use the information to design and construct a simple instrument to keep track of the daytime hours.

Day and Night and the Seasons

Day and Night

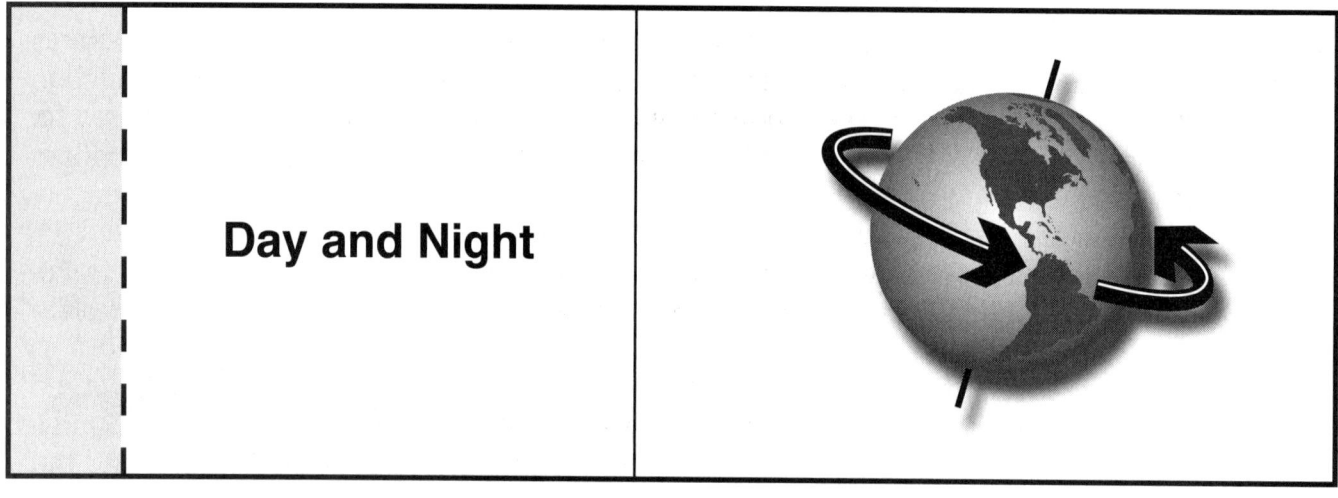

Summer Solstice

The Sun's Rays During Summer in the Northern Hemisphere

Winter Solstice

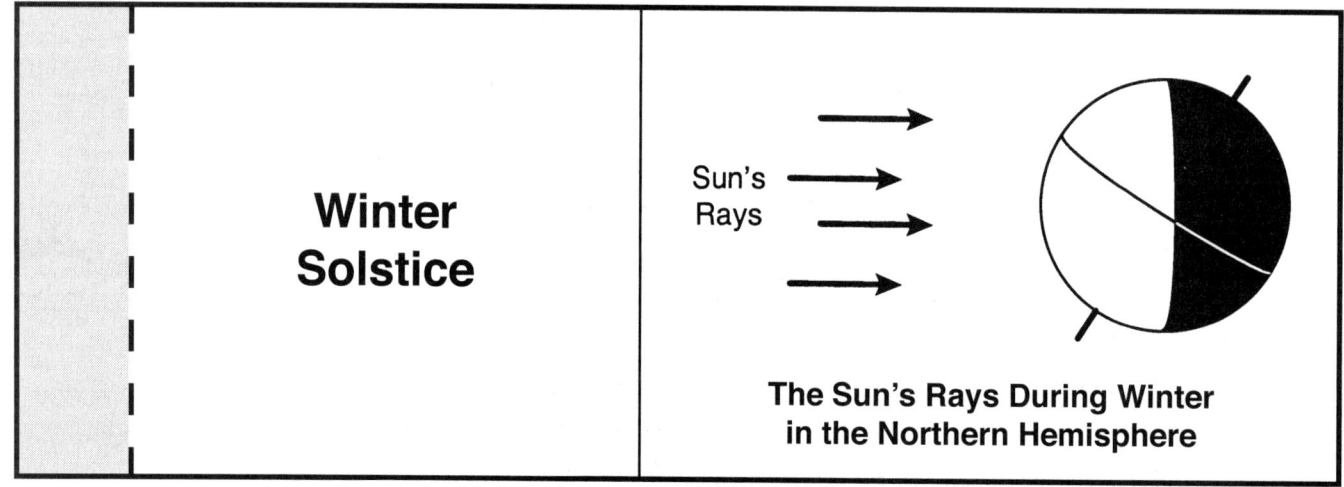

The Sun's Rays During Winter in the Northern Hemisphere

Interactive Notebook: Earth & Space Science   Astronomy: The Moon—Mini-Lesson

The Moon

Mini-Lesson

Read the following information. Then cut out and attach this box to the right-hand page of your science notebook. Use what you have learned to create the left-hand page.

A **satellite** is a small body that orbits around a larger body. Earth has one natural satellite, the **moon**. The moon orbits Earth once every 27.3 days. It is our closest neighbor at 384,000 km (239,000 miles). The moon's diameter is 3,476 km (2,160 miles) compared to Earth's diameter of 12,756 km (7,926 miles). The moon is one of the largest satellites in the solar system.

The moon's mass is a little over one one-hundredth (0.0124) that of Earth's, and its gravitational pull is one-sixth the pull of gravity on Earth. As a result, there is no air on the moon. However, the moon's gravity causes tides on Earth; it causes the water in the oceans to rise and fall twice daily.

Many of the moon's features can be seen through binoculars and small telescopes. The most obvious features on the lunar surface are the **maria**. These are large, dark areas that were mistaken for seas and oceans by early observers. The moon's surface is also covered with **craters**. Craters are roughly circular, bowl-shaped holes. It is thought that the craters were formed by the impacts of vast numbers of rocky bodies that crashed into the moon's surface during its early history.

Daily observations of the moon reveal a slight change in the moon's appearance from one day to the next. These changes are due to the rotation of the moon around the earth and the earth's rotation around the sun. These changes are known as the **phases of the moon**.

Phases of the Moon

New Moon | Waxing Crescent | First Quarter

Waxing Gibbous | Full Moon | Waning Gibbous

Last Quarter | Waning Crescent | New Moon

How to Create Your Left-Hand Notebook Page

Complete the following steps to create the left-hand page of your science notebook. Use lots of color.

Step 1: Cut out the title and glue it to the top of the notebook page.
Step 2: Cut out the flap chart. Apply glue to the back of the gray tab and attach the chart below the title. Write the correct definition under each flap.
Step 3: Cut out the diagram box. Apply glue to the back and attach the box at the bottom of the page. Shade each circle to illustrate the correct moon phase.

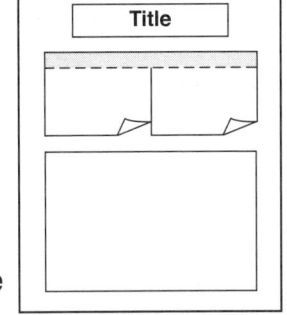

Demonstrate What You Have Learned

Create a model illustrating the phases of the moon. Separate four cream-filled chocolate sandwich cookies. Scrape away the frosting to represent each phase of the moon. Glue the cookie halves in a circle to a paper plate. Label each phase.

The Moon

Features of the Moon

Maria | Craters

Phases of the Moon as Seen From Earth

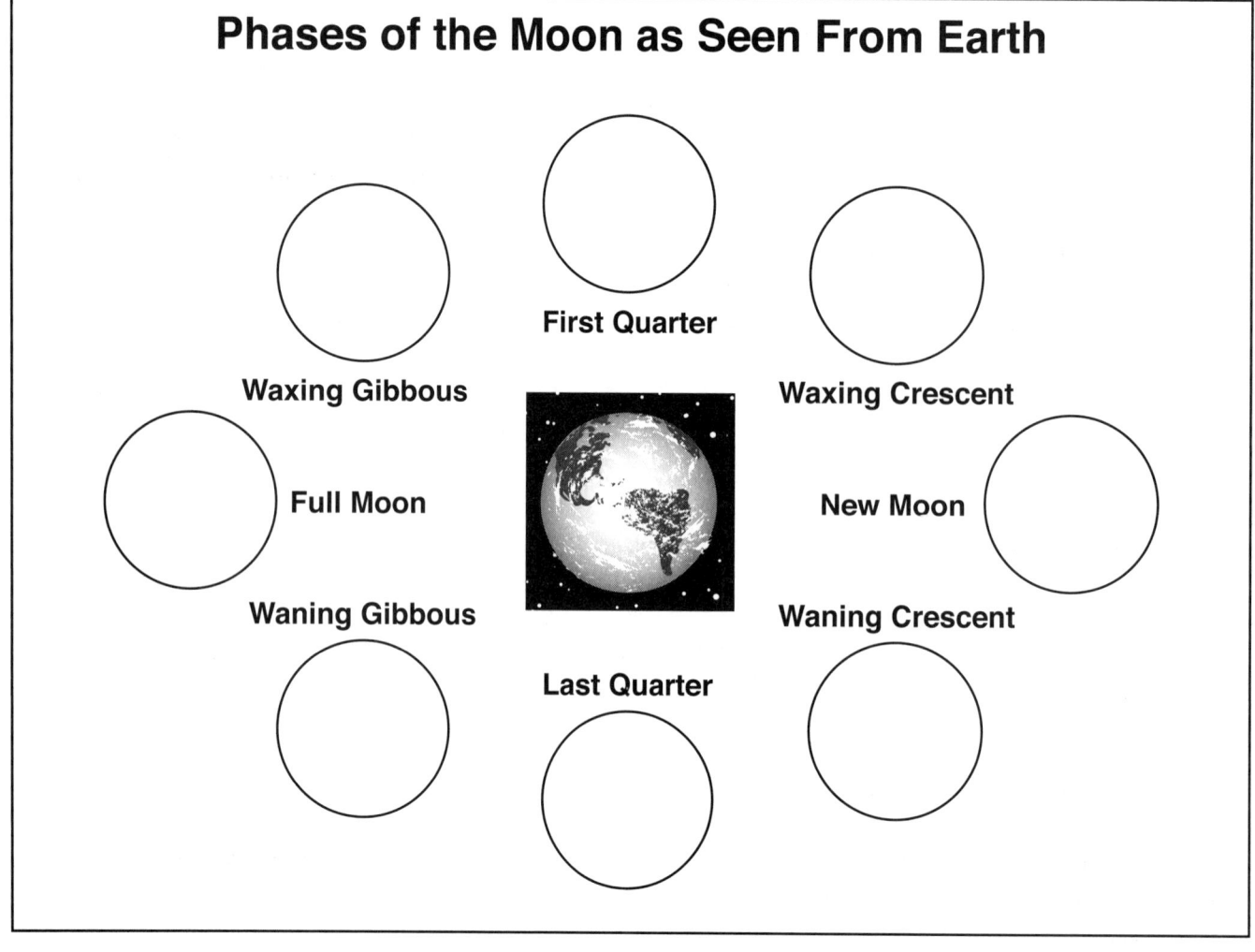

- Waxing Gibbous
- First Quarter
- Waxing Crescent
- Full Moon
- New Moon
- Waning Gibbous
- Last Quarter
- Waning Crescent

Solar and Lunar Eclipses

Mini-Lesson

Read the following information. Then cut out and attach this box to the right-hand page of your science notebook. Use what you have learned to create the left-hand page.

A **solar eclipse** is a blackout of the sun's light when the moon passes between Earth and the sun. The moon's shadow extends all the way to Earth and causes a brief period of darkness for people who are under it. The moon's shadow is small, only an area about 273 km wide. As Earth rotates, the shadow appears to move across the surface of the earth. At any one position, a solar eclipse only lasts for a few minutes. A solar eclipse can only occur during a new moon. However, we do not have an eclipse every time there is a new moon because the moon's orbit is tilted at about 5° with respect to Earth's orbit. Only at certain new moons is the moon aligned just right in its orbit to pass exactly between Earth and the sun.

When the full moon moves into the shadow of Earth, we experience a **lunar eclipse**. Because Earth's shadow is so large, a lunar eclipse can be seen from the entire dark side of the earth. Also, because Earth's shadow is so large, lunar eclipses can last up to about 100 minutes. If only a portion of the moon is eclipsed, the eclipse is called a **partial lunar eclipse**. A lunar eclipse can only occur during a full moon. However, we do not have a lunar eclipse during every full moon because the moon's axis is tilted. Only at certain full moons is the moon aligned just right in its orbit around Earth to result in an eclipse.

How to Create Your Left-Hand Notebook Page

Complete the following steps to create the left-hand page of your science notebook. Use lots of color.

Step 1: Cut out the title and glue it to the top of the page.
Step 2: Cut out the flap chart. Apply glue to the back of the gray center section and attach the chart below the title.
Step 3: Draw the correct eclipse in each box on the chart. Explain the location of the sun, moon, and Earth under each flap.

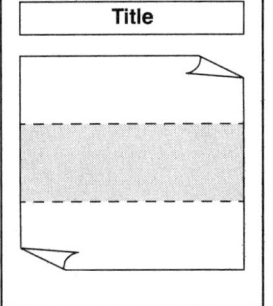

Demonstrate What You Have Learned

Create a three-dimensional model of the Sun-Earth-Moon system and use it to demonstrate what happens during both a lunar and solar eclipse.

Solar and Lunar Eclipses

Solar Eclipse

Sun-Earth-Moon System

Lunar Eclipse

Objects in Space

Mini-Lesson

Read the following information. Then cut out and attach this box to the right-hand page of your science notebook. Use what you have learned to create the left-hand page.

Astronomers believe that our solar system is surrounded by a "cloud" of comets at distances far beyond the orbit of Pluto. Normally, they stay in this region. A **comet** is a compact chunk of frozen gases and dust. They have been described as "dirty snowballs." Most comets are thought to be only a few kilometers in diameter. They follow long, elliptical orbits about the sun. But from time to time, they sweep around the narrow end of their orbits near the sun. When this happens, they provide a spectacular sight for a short time. Perhaps the most famous comet is Comet Halley. It has an orbit period of 76 years. It is predicted to appear again in 2061.

Small sand- to boulder-sized particles of space debris called **meteoroids** travel in the solar system. Large meteoroids are believed to come from the asteroid belt; other meteoroids have their origins in comets. When a meteoroid enters Earth's atmosphere, it begins to burn and starts to glow. The meteoroid is now referred to as **meteor**. A "falling star," is actually a meteor. When a large meteoroid does not burn up completely in the atmosphere and strikes the surface of the earth, it is referred to as a **meteorite**.

Stars are found in clustered groups called **galaxies**. Some of them are giant spirals, some of them are shaped like ellipses, and others are irregular in shape. We live in a large spiral galaxy called the **Milky Way**.

Constellations are groups of stars imagined to form figures or designs in the night sky. They were given names by early Greek astronomers after animals, mythological characters, or familiar objects. Astronomers officially recognize a total of 88 constellations. The constellations we can see depend on the time of night, time of year, and where on Earth we live. Constellations are not seen in the exact same place in the sky all night. They seem to move across the night sky because Earth is rotating on its axis. Different constellations are visible at different times of the year. Also, constellations seen from the Northern Hemisphere are different from those seen from the Southern Hemisphere.

How to Create Your Left-Hand Notebook Page

Complete the following steps to create the left-hand page of your science notebook. Use lots of color.

Step 1: Cut out the title and glue it to the top of the notebook page.
Step 2: Cut out the four flap charts. Apply glue to the back of each gray tab and attach the charts below the title.
Step 3: Write the correct definition under each flap.

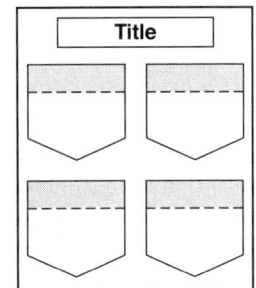

Demonstrate What You Have Learned

Observe a meteor shower. Check the American Meteor Calendar at <www.amsmeteors.org/meteor-showers/meteor-shower-calendar> to find the best time and date to view a meteor shower in your area. Record your observations in your science notebook.

Objects in Space

Comet

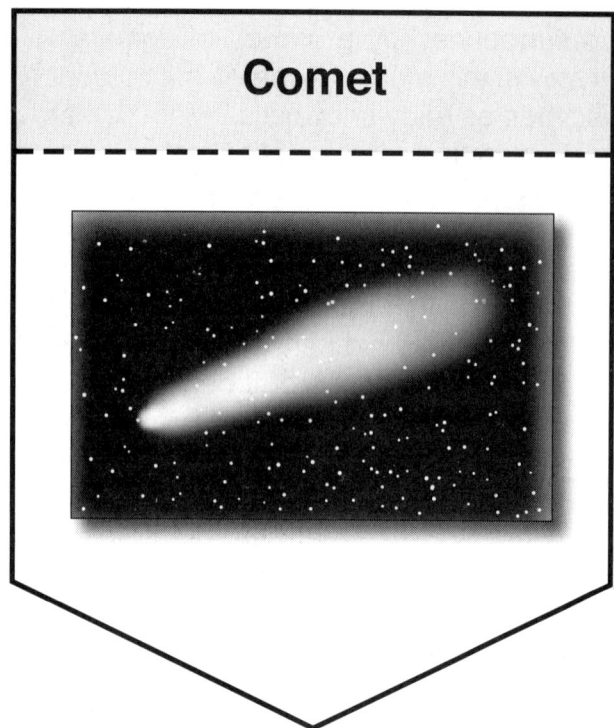

Meteoroid, Meteor, and Meteorite

Constellation

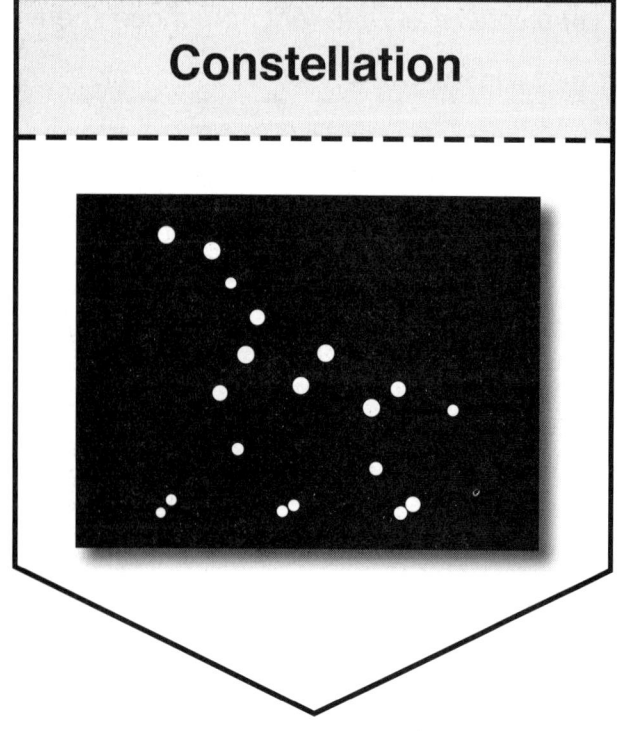

Galaxy

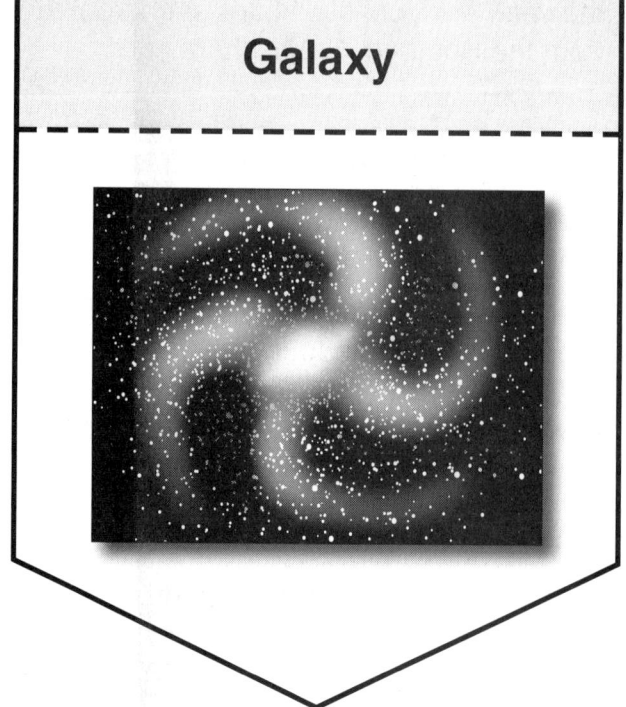